JACKIE GREEN
LAUREN GREEN MCAFEE

D1531976

How One Ordinary Life Can
Make an Eternal Difference

legacy

LifeWay Press® Nashville, Tennessee

Published by LifeWay Press®
© 2019 Jackie Green and Lauren Green McAfee

ISBN: 978-1-5359-5878-3
Item: 005815392
Dewey decimal classification: 248.843
Subject heading: WOMEN \ CHARACTER \ WOMEN IN THE BIBLE

Unless otherwise noted, all Scripture quotations are taken from the Christian Standard Bible®, Copyright © 2017 by Holman Bible Publishers˚. Used by permission. Christian Standard Bible˚ and CSB˚ are federally registered trademarks of Holman Bible Publishers. Scripture quotations marked (ESV) are from the ESV® Bible (The Holy Bible, English Standard Version®), copyright © 2001 by Crossway, a publishing ministry of Good News Publishers. Used by permission. All rights reserved. Scripture quotations marked (NIV) are taken from the Holy Bible, New International Version®, NIV®. Copyright © 1973, 1978, 1984, 2011 by Biblica, Inc.™ Used by permission of Zondervan. All rights reserved worldwide. www.zondervan.com. The "NIV" and "New International Version" are trademarks registered in the United States Patent and Trademark Office by Biblica, Inc.™ Scripture quotations from THE MESSAGE. Copyright © by Eugene H. Peterson 1993, 1994, 1995, 1996, 2000, 2001, 2002. Used by permission of NavPress. All rights reserved. Represented by Tyndale House Publishers, Inc. Scriptures marked NLT are taken from the Holy Bible, New Living Translation (NLT), copyright © 1996, 2004, 2007, 2013, 2015 by Tyndale House Foundation. Used by permission of Tyndale House Publishers, Inc., Carol Stream, IL 60188. All rights reserved. Scripture quotations marked (AMP) are taken from the Amplified Bible, Copyright © 1954, 1958, 1962, 1964, 1965, 1987 by The Lockman Foundation. Used by permission.

To order additional copies of this resource, write LifeWay Church Resources Customer Service; One LifeWay Plaza; Nashville, TN 37234; Fax orders to 615.251.5933; call toll-free 800.458.2772; email orderentry@lifeway.com; order online at www.LifeWay.com; or visit the LifeWay Christian Store serving you.

Printed in Canada.

Adult Ministry Publishing, LifeWay Church Resources, One LifeWay Plaza, Nashville, TN 37234

Authors are represented by Alive Literary Agency, 7680 Goddard Street, Suite 200, Colorado Springs, CO, 80920. www.aliveliterary.com

EDITORIAL TEAM, ADULT MINISTRY PUBLISHING

Faith Whatley
Director, Adult Ministry

Michelle Hicks
Manager, Adult Ministry
Short Term Bible Studies

Mike Wakefield
Content Editor

Emily Chadwell
Production Editor

Heather Wetherington
Art Director

Chelsea Waack
Graphic Designer

Jennifer Allison
Cover Design

Jennifer Denning & Donna McKinney
Bible Study Development

TABLE OF CONTENTS

ABOUT THE AUTHORS

Jackie Green wears many different hats as she navigates writing, speaking, organizing events for women, being a wife and mother to six and GiGi to four. She is the co-founder of Museum of the Bible and serves on the board of several organizations. She is also the founder of Women of Legacy—an effort to help women discover and leave an eternal legacy. She has been married for thirty-five years to her husband, Steve, whom she actively supports in his role as President of Hobby Lobby and Chairman of the Board at Museum of the Bible. She has co-authored two books: *This Dangerous Book* with her husband, Steve Green, and *Only One Life* with her daughter, Lauren Green McAfee. Although she enjoys traveling and meeting people worldwide, her favorite place to be is home with her family. Connect with Jackie at www.jackiegreen.us.

Lauren Green McAfee is a communicator, connector, and coffee enthusiast with a heart to engage others with the Bible. While earning her graduate degrees in pastoral counseling and theology, Lauren worked for her father, Steve Green, as he founded Museum of the Bible in Washington, D.C. Today, Lauren works at the Hobby Lobby corporate office and pursues a PhD in ethics and public policy at Southern Baptist Theological Seminary. Connect with Lauren at laurenamcafee.com and on Instagram: @laurenmacafee.

INTRODUCTION

You were created by God to impact others with your life.

God used women throughout the Bible to accomplish His purposes, and He continues to use women today to advance His kingdom. In the pages of this study, we will share inspiring stories of women who made an impact. But shaping a powerful legacy is not just for the elite few.

So what is "legacy"? Think of legacy as that which lives on beyond you. And realize it is a story that you are writing daily, even in the mundane.

My (Jackie) grandmother-in-law, and my (Lauren) great-grandmother, Marie Green, often quoted to her family a line from a poem by the missionary C. T. Studd. The portion she emphasized was, "Only one life, 'twill soon be past, Only what's done for Christ will last."[1]

We are grateful to be in a family that has intentionally shaped our legacy for generations. We are beneficiaries of this legacy, and we pray we are faithful to continue living it with intentionality.

You don't have to come from a family with a kingdom legacy to dive into the adventure of shaping your own. Each of us, regardless of our circumstances and context, has the opportunity to know God better and to use our influence to make Him known.

Women of legacy understand that our victories can and do impact countless others, including generations yet to be born. So, together, let's be a generation of legacy-building leaders, spending our one life using our gifts and strengths in His service. Because only what's done for Christ will last.

Jackie + Lauren

session one:

COURAGE
& FAITH

WATCH

To watch the free video of Session One, go to LifeWay.com/LegacyStudy.

DISCUSS

What is one thing that stood out to you from the video? *Museum of the Bible*

What do you think it would have been like to live in the time of Jesus? *Difficult, Scary*

Do you have faith to believe that God can make seemingly impossible things happen in your life? Explain.

How have you seen God do the impossible?

Would you say you're a person of courage and faith? Why or why not?

How have you seen someone step out in courageous faith? Is God currently calling you to do that?

9-37

INTRODUCTION

"Faith does not eliminate questions. But faith knows where to take them."[2]
ELISABETH ELLIOT

In 1955, Jim Elliot, Peter Fleming, and Ed McCully, who were all—along with their wives—missionaries in Ecuador, felt compelled by God to bring the gospel to the Waodani Indians (known as the "Auca Indians" at the time).[3] The Waodani were an unreached people group located in the Andes Mountains. This tribe had little or no contact with the civilized world, and its members were known to be very violent. But the missionaries' calling from God and compulsion to reach the lost for Christ superseded any fear they had.

These three men teamed up with Nate Saint, a pilot for Missionary Aviation Fellowship, and began to take small steps to reach the Waodani. For three months they made flights over the village, dropping gifts and supplies in the hopes that their efforts would build trust and eventual friendship. On Tuesday, January 3, 1956, the men decided to land the plane on a river sandbar about four miles from the tribe. They also invited Roger Youderian, another missionary working with native Indians in South America, to join them. They set up camp and began to fly over the village, inviting the tribe to meet them. On Friday morning, they had their first visitors. Though this encounter was encouraging, by Saturday afternoon their wives back at the mission station lost all contact with them. Eventually, the wives learned that a group of the tribe members had come back to the missionaries' camp on Saturday morning and killed all five men by spearing them to death.[4] It seemed their courageous actions had a tragic end.

But the story wasn't over.

After Jim's death, his wife, Elisabeth, and their 10-month-old daughter, Valerie, stayed in Ecuador to continue mission work with the Quichua Indians, a tribe she and Jim worked with prior to his attempt to reach the Waodani. While continuing this work after her husband's death, Elisabeth providentially met two runaway Waodani women, who ended up living with her for a year. These two women became the key to opening the door for Elisabeth to work with the tribe who killed her husband and the other four missionaries.[5] Elisabeth and her young daughter entered the Waodani village and began to share the gospel. Joining her in this missionary effort was Rachel Saint, Nate Saint's sister. These two women had the courage and faith to live among and share the gospel with those who had taken the lives of their loved ones. During their time with the tribe, Elisabeth and Rachel saw many Waodani come to saving faith in Jesus Christ, including the men who killed the missionaries. What a legacy of courage and faith these men and women left behind!

While most of us know and understand the call we have to go into all the world and make disciples, too many of us never fulfill that call because of fear. But Paul said we have not been given a "spirit of fear, but one of power, love, and sound judgment" (2 Tim. 1:7). We will never share the gospel, stand for truth, or contend for the faith the way God has called us to if fear rules our hearts. We must move forward in courage and faith, empowered by the Holy Spirit, with our eyes on Jesus. That's a legacy worth following.

> Think of a time you wrestled between fear and courage. Which did you choose, and what was the tipping point?

> How did your faith play a part?

DAY 1 **COURAGE: ESTHER**

A QUEEN WITH A SECRET
Go back in time almost five hundred years before the birth of Christ and you'll find a woman who struggled between fear and courage. The danger was real and the stakes were high. But to grasp the full fear she faced, you have to begin with her backstory. It started in 483 BC, over one hundred years after the Jews were taken into Babylonian captivity.[6] One group of exiles had returned to Jerusalem, but more remained even after Babylon fell in 539 BC.

Some Jews wound up in Persia, which rose as the dominant kingdom in the Middle East after Babylon's fall. There, Xerxes the Great (also known as King Ahasuerus) ruled from 486 to 465 BC.[7] Arrogant and impulsive, the king forever banished his queen, Vashti, from his presence when she refused his request to appear before his guests at a banquet to display her beauty (Esth. 1). The king searched for Vashti's replacement from among the most beautiful girls in his kingdom and chose Esther as his new queen (Esth. 2). What Esther kept secret was that she was a Jewish exile and orphan, raised by her cousin Mordecai.

One day, a conflict arose between Mordecai and Haman. Haman was a nobleman the king had honored who expected all the royal officials at the king's gate to kneel before him, and Mordecai was the only official who refused. Learning that Mordecai was a Jew, Haman schemed to kill not only Mordecai but all the Jews in the kingdom (Esth. 3). He convinced the king to issue an edict that on a given date about a year in the future, all Jewish men, women, and children in the kingdom were to be killed (Esth. 4).

Read Esther 4:1-8. What emotions do you see portrayed by Mordecai and Esther based on the news they received in this passage?

Read Esther 4:8-12. What specifically did Mordecai ask Esther to do and what was her response?

Mordecai knew Esther held a place of influence before the king and he wanted her to leverage that influence to save her people. But Esther knew it wasn't as simple as strolling into the throne room and making a request. Approaching the king without being summoned was likely signing her own death warrant.

Fear initially kept Esther from taking the necessary steps to help her people. At this point she put preserving her own life above saving her fellow countrymen.

What do you think Esther expected Mordecai to say or do when she explained her situation in verse 11?

THE VOICE OF FEAR

Esther wasn't just being a drama queen. Her life truly would be in jeopardy if she approached the king at her own initiative. And his reputation as a despot not to be crossed was well established. So her fear was genuine and valid. The worst possible scenario was whispering in her ear, and it was hard to ignore.

No doubt, you've heard the voice of fear. It says the task in front of you is impossible. It says you're not smart enough for your job, and soon everyone is going to discover how incapable you really are. It tells you your boss is going to fire you or your husband is going to leave you. When you should be sleeping, fear reminds you of your manager who intimidates you or the bills you can't pay. And when you find yourself living the day-after-day struggle of loving a prodigal child or fighting cancer or caring for an aging parent, fear greets you every morning with the unwelcome forecast that today will be worse than yesterday, and things won't get better anytime soon.

Fear plays a broken record in your mind of all the worst possible outcomes. Fear takes your emotions hostage. It sabotages your body with sweaty palms, a racing heart, trembling limbs, and a gnawing in your gut. If you listen to fear, it will tell you to run when you should take a stand. It will urge you to keep quiet when you should speak up. Fear will prompt you to quit when you should stay, and linger when you should leave. It's no wonder the Bible addresses the topic of fear so much. Over three hundred times God commanded us in so many words to *stop being afraid!*[8]

How has fear negatively affected your decision making?

When have you most recently allowed fear to consume you and spiritually paralyze you?

CHOOSING COURAGE OVER FEAR

God speaks to us through His Word, but sometimes He also speaks to us through other people. In Esther's case, it was Mordecai who challenged her to choose courage over her fear.

Read Esther 4:13-14. Write out Mordecai's response to Esther in your own words.

Mordecai redirected Esther to focus on God's calling and purpose for her life rather than the difficulty that was before her.

When you know God has called you to a purpose, you can step into that role—no matter how frightening—because you are confident that God is in control. Fear may not disappear, but that's when courage becomes stronger than fear.

Esther had reason to be afraid. She probably thought, *Who am I to intervene and save my people from Haman's slaughter? I don't even belong in the palace to begin with. If these people knew who I really am, they'd know I'm not qualified to be here. They'd throw me out.* She truly had done nothing in her own ability to become queen. Mordecai rightly understood Esther was where she was at that moment in time because God had placed her there by divine appointment.

> How has God positioned you where you are in life "for such a time as this"? What people are depending on your courage?

> What is God calling you to say or do that requires you to move outside your comfort zone?

"IF I PERISH, I PERISH."

Courage takes action to do the right thing without always having the assurance that everything will turn out OK. And honestly, things don't always turn out OK. Sometimes the courageous suffer, hurt, or lose. Sometimes they die in the battle. No person better exemplifies courage than Jesus Christ, who, knowing the agony that lay ahead, steadfastly pursued God's purpose for Him to die for the sins of the world. Jesus took the path of courage to meet our dire need, notwithstanding the personal risk or cost to Himself.

In what sense are you standing in the legacy of Jesus' courage?

The legacy of courage you leave to someone who follows in your path might begin the day you stand up to do the right thing, or the day you walk away from the wrong thing.

When have you seen someone demonstrate courage by standing up to do what's right? By walking away from what's wrong?

Are you currently facing a situation where God is calling you to take one of these courageous steps? Explain.

If you're not currently facing such a situation, at some point you will. Don't let fear win the day. Don't let Satan use his favorite weapon to paralyze you. Rather, listen to the voice of the Father saying, "Take heart. Fear not. Be strong and courageous." Trust Him and move forward.

IN YOUR OWN WORDS: Based on what you've studied today, how would you define courage?

IN YOUR OWN LIFE: Based on what you've learned today, what is the next step God is challenging you to take toward building a legacy of courage?

DAY 2 **COURAGE: ESTHER**

"A ship in harbor is safe, but that is not what ships are built for."[9]

JOHN A. SHEDD

Courage marks the heroes and heroines of our favorite stories. Whether from the Bible, childhood fairy tales, or modern movies, we love those ordinary people who boldly take a stand to face down life's "giants."

What is it exactly that qualifies some people as exceptionally courageous? Clinical psychologist Melanie Greenberg, PhD, identifies six distinct ways we characterize courage:

1. Feeling fear yet choosing to act

2. Following your heart

3. Persevering in the face of adversity

4. Standing up for what is right

5. Expanding your horizons; letting go of the familiar

6. Facing suffering with dignity or faith[10]

As you study Esther's story again today, consider which of these characteristics of courage she demonstrated. Ask yourself: *Which ones do I need to cultivate?*

JUST SAY NO?
Skim Esther 4:5-11 from yesterday's study to recall Mordecai's request of Esther and her hesitation.

Esther already had reason to feel she didn't belong and wasn't entitled to be queen. She held a secret: She was a Jew in exile and an orphan, living in a Persian palace in the role of queen. Now she was facing a bully determined to murder the cousin who raised her and wipe out all her people. The clock was ticking. And her cousin, Mordecai, asked her to go before the king and plead for mercy to save the Jews. But there were so many reasons not to.

Put yourself in Esther's place. What might be some of the reasons not to comply with Mordecai's request?

Lots of reasons probably went through Esther's head. She'd have to reveal her identity. She could be banished from the court. Haman could take revenge on her. She could be executed. She could fail.

INSIDE AND OUTSIDE THE ZONE

Regardless of the reasons, Esther needed to move from her safe spot to take action. She needed to step outside her comfort zone to make a difference. It would take courage.

How would you define "comfort zone"? How easily do you move outside of yours?

Feel safe

What is something God is calling you to do that will require you to step outside of that zone?

NOW OR LATER

When it comes to parenting, we sometimes hear about aiming for "first-time obedience" or "immediate obedience." The point is, the parent shouldn't have to ask twice; the child should immediately carry out what he or she has been told to do. Esther did what Mordecai asked, but she didn't jump right up and run to the king's chambers. In fact, she did all these things first:

- Called on all the Jews to fast and pray for her for three days (4:15-16);

- Approached the king and invited him and Haman to a banquet the same day (5:1-4);

- At that banquet, invited the king and Haman to another banquet the next day (5:5-8).

Was Esther procrastinating? Or was she being smart and deliberate in planning her strategy?

Wine banquets.

There is a difference between being courageous and being careless. Endless deliberation can become simple procrastination that prevents us from ever taking action. On the other hand, there is a place for adequate prayer, planning, and preparation.

Read Esther 7:1-6a. What actions did Esther take that were surely outside her comfort zone?

Petition – Idea Life
Request – Life of her people

NO TURNING BACK

When fear tells us to play it safe, God calls us to choose courage and step outside our comfort zone to do what is right. To answer God's call and choose courage is to walk right into the thing we fear regardless of the cost. Courage keeps us moving toward obedience, trembling but resolute.

Consider Isaiah's prophecy concerning Jesus and the courageous obedience He would display in the face of suffering. Underline any phrase below that shows determination to obey God in the face of terror. Circle the one that most inspires you to emulate His courage.

"The Lord God has opened my ear,
and I was not rebellious;
I did not turn back.
I gave my back to those who beat me,
and my cheeks to those
who tore out my beard.
I did not hide my face from scorn and spitting.
The Lord God will help me;
therefore I have not been humiliated;
therefore I have set my face like flint,
and I know I will not be put to shame."
ISAIAH 50:5-7

Read Esther 7:6b-10. When Esther acted with courage, what happened to the things she might have feared, such as revealing her identity, Haman's revenge, being banished, and being executed?

The God who calls us to courageous obedience does not leave us to succeed or fail on our own. He is the same God who promises, "I am with you always" (Matt. 28:20). As we obey, He acts to do what only He can do. He can engineer the outcome of circumstances and the timing of events (Ex. 14; Josh. 10:1-15). He can sway people's hearts (Gen. 39:21; Ex. 3:21; 9:12; 10:1,27; 11:10; 12:36; 14:8; Josh. 11:20). He can solve problems in ways we could never imagine. When we see no possible solution, He makes a way. Ours is a mountain-moving God (Job 9:4-5).

FINAL IMPACT

Esther now stood in an in-between place. With Haman out of the picture, it was like a movie where the danger seems to be over, but then you realize it's not. She had delivered her message unscathed. But there was still an irreversible decree quickly approaching. The king's order had been given to kill all Jews in the kingdom on the thirteenth day of the twelfth month, the month of Adar (3:12-13). Once the king issued a decree sealed with his signet ring, it could not be revoked. The clock was ticking, and even King Xerxes couldn't stop his own decree.

Would Esther risk everything to do the right thing—the courageous thing—and still fail to accomplish what she set out to do? Success is not always guaranteed to the courageous. But it's nearly impossible to make an impact, indeed to leave a legacy, if we don't move outside our comfort zone. Esther chapters 8–10 reveal how Esther's courageous actions did succeed and establish a legacy in the process.

Here's how events unfolded:

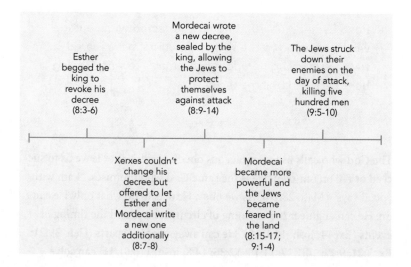

| Esther begged the king to revoke his decree (8:3-6) | Mordecai wrote a new decree, sealed by the king, allowing the Jews to protect themselves against attack (8:9-14) | The Jews struck down their enemies on the day of attack, killing five hundred men (9:5-10) |
| Xerxes couldn't change his decree but offered to let Esther and Mordecai write a new one additionally (8:7-8) | Mordecai became more powerful and the Jews became feared in the land (8:15-17; 9:1-4) |

Esther not only survived but gained respect and reward for her bravery. More than that, Esther's willingness to risk her life to save her people left a legacy that long outlived her. On the two days following the attack, the Jews rested and celebrated with a day of feasting and joy (9:17). Those two days became an annual celebration of feasting and gift giving to commemorate the time when the Jews escaped slaughter at the hands of their enemies. The feast was named "Purim," which means 'lots,' a reference to the lots Haman cast to determine which day he would have the Jews slaughtered (3:7).[11]

> "The Jews bound themselves, their descendants, and all who joined with them to a commitment that they would not fail to celebrate these two days each and every year according to the written instructions and according to the time appointed. These days are remembered and celebrated by every generation, family, province, and city, so that these days of Purim will not lose their significance in Jewish life and their memory will not fade from their descendants."
> **ESTHER 9:27-28**

Esther's legacy lives to this day as Jews still celebrate Purim. Your brave steps, big and small, will also leave a legacy of courage for those who come behind you.

IN YOUR OWN WORDS: Based on what you've studied today, how would you further define courage?

IN YOUR OWN LIFE: What big or small steps of courage is God calling you to take today?

DAY 3 FAITH: MARY, MOTHER OF JESUS

"A man of courage is also full of faith."[12]
MARCUS TULLIUS CICERO

FAITH TAKES COURAGE

Addressing the Cornell University graduating class of 2008, Pulitzer Prize-nominated writer, actress, and civil rights activist Maya Angelou argued that courage is the most important virtue because without it no other virtue can be practiced consistently.

Drawing on her years of experience, the then eighty-year-old Angelou said, "You can be kind and true and fair and generous and just, and even merciful, occasionally. But to be that thing time after time, you have to really have courage."[13]

Do you agree? Disagree? How does it take courage to practice consistently some of the other virtues covered in this Bible study?
Boldness?

Compassion?

Tenacity?

Loyalty?

Prayerfulness?

(Faithfulness in) Witnessing?

Faith?

In the next two days, we'll look at the virtue of faith in the example of Mary, the mother of Jesus. As we do, consider how it takes courage to believe God and obey Him when you don't have all the facts and you don't know how everything will turn out. Ask yourself: *What was the legacy Mary left by her simple faith? And what will mine be?*

A PRIOR ANGELIC VISIT
Read Luke 1:26-30.

In verse 26, Luke notes that the angelic visit to Mary comes "in the sixth month." The context for this time reference is from the passage immediately preceding (vv. 5-25), where we learn that Mary's older cousin, Elizabeth, who was barren, had miraculously conceived and was expecting her first baby. Elizabeth was then in "the sixth month" of her pregnancy (v. 36). This is significant for a couple of reasons besides the relationship between Mary and Elizabeth. For one thing, God was laying out the plan for the entry of His Son into the world. Elizabeth's baby would be John the Baptist, the one who would go before the Messiah to prepare people to turn their hearts toward Him.

But there's another interesting connection to Mary in Elizabeth's back story. It has to do with how Elizabeth and her husband got the news that they were expecting. Long before sonograms, social media posts, and gender reveal parties, news about these sorts of things traveled much slower, so maybe Mary had heard, and maybe she hadn't. But when Elizabeth's husband, Zechariah, got the news of his wife's pregnancy, he had trouble believing it even though it was announced by an angel.

Zechariah was a priest serving in the temple on the day Gabriel appeared to tell him the good news that Elizabeth would bear him a son. But Zechariah doubted: "How can I know this?" he contended. "For I am an old man, and my wife is well along in years" (1:18). Because of Zechariah's unbelief, the messenger of God struck him mute until the day of John's birth. As previously noted, news traveled much slower then. Mary may or may not have known how her cousin's husband was suffering for his unbelief. But in putting Zechariah's encounter with the angel Gabriel just before Mary's in his Gospel, Luke gave us a striking juxtaposition between how two different people handled the challenge of trusting God with things they could not understand or explain.

GABRIEL RETURNS

As we just noted, Gabriel's visit to Mary wasn't his first trip to earth. He had visited Zechariah six months prior, and hundreds of years earlier he had appeared to the prophet Daniel (Dan. 8:15-17; 9:21). He always came to deliver important messages from God. But this angelic visit was a first for young Mary, and Gabriel's appearance must have stunned her, to say the least.

From Luke 1:26-27, list at least three things you know about Mary:

1. Virgin
2. Highly favored
3. Courage

In Mary's day, girls typically got engaged in their early teens. Mary could have been as young as thirteen at the time.

What were you doing in your early teens? What were your interests? What occupied most of your time?

If you've been engaged, what plans were you making during that time?

While your teen years and Mary's would have probably been quite different, life appeared to be going along as planned for an ordinary girl in a small Palestinian town until Gabriel showed up.

Why do you think Mary was deeply troubled by Gabriel's greeting? Was her fear justified? Explain.

"OKAY, BUT HOW?"
Read Luke 1:31-34.

When Gabriel started giving Mary the details of her future, the words must have come across as incredible. Put yourselves in her shoes. What would you have thought? Probably something like: *This can't be real. Is this really happening? Nobody knows the future. Really???*

Mary asked, "How can this be?" It was a natural question. But why was she not rebuked as Zechariah was (1:19-20)? Mary's question was one of wonder and clarification, whereas Zechariah's was one of doubt. No virgin had ever become pregnant before, let alone with the Savior of the world! It was impossible. It simply didn't occur within the realm of natural events. How could it be?

What's one thing God has promised in Scripture that you can't comprehend how He will accomplish?

Check out Gabriel's response in Luke 1:35-37.

If we had been in Mary's shoes, we might have persisted with, "Could you break that down a little further, please? Put it in plain English (or Aramaic). Explain so I can understand how the Holy Spirit is going to come upon me, and the power of the Most High overshadow me, and I will end up pregnant." But the incarnation doesn't make sense to our limited understanding. That God Almighty became a man and was born as a human baby shatters the laws of nature and defies human comprehension. In the end, how God would accomplish it was not the point. All Mary needed to know was what God had demonstrated with Elizabeth and Zechariah, which Gabriel stated in verse 37.

Write verse 37 here:

When have you seen God accomplish what you knew to be humanly impossible?

ARE YOU IN?

Sure, it's great to hear that you're highly favored with God and you've been selected for a special project. At least it's great while you're alone talking with the angel. But what's it going to be like when you're back with your family and friends and your belly starts to grow? People start to stare and whisper. Your fiancé doubts your faithfulness and feels betrayed. Your own family members look at you differently. Pregnancy for an unmarried girl in that time likely meant losing her fiancé, family, and reputation. Attributing the pregnancy to the Holy Spirit could make Mary sound like a lunatic.[14]

Mary didn't ask for this to happen. Gabriel delivered the message and Mary responded with faith. She was confronted with a socially unacceptable situation, and while she may have had feelings of fear and doubt, she did not rely on those feelings to determine her response. She relied on her trust and faith in God.

Read 1:38 and write Mary's response in your own words.

Are you currently facing life situations that require you to rely on what you know to be true about God because your feelings don't match that truth? Explain.

GOD-PLEASING FAITH

"Now without faith it is impossible to please God."
HEBREWS 11:6

Hebrews 11:1 describes faith as "the reality of what is hoped for, the proof of what is not seen." Faith is about trusting God when we don't have all the answers and nothing adds up. We believe Him not because we see the clear explanation; we believe Him even when there is no explanation. Faith is trusting without seeing.

This is precisely the kind of faith Jesus encouraged in Mark 9:14-27. The father of a demon-possessed boy brought his son to Jesus and said, "If you can do anything, have compassion on us and help us" (v. 22). Jesus responded, "'If you can'? Everything is possible for the one who believes" (v. 23). And the father cried out, "I do believe; help my unbelief!" (v. 24).

What is God challenging you to believe right now?
What is He calling you to do?

How would you gauge your faith in this moment? Who
are you more like?
☐ Zechariah—filled with questions and doubt
☐ Father of the boy—believing but struggling to fully
believe
☐ Mary—all in, full of faith

Explain your choice:

It's easy to believe God can do the impossible—until the impossible work of God involves a personal step of faith from you. But the powerful God who called an ordinary girl to be a part of His extraordinary plan is the same powerful God calling you. He will accomplish it. Don't miss what He's wanting to do in and through you.

IN YOUR OWN WORDS: Based on what you've studied today, how would you define faith?

Believe when don't understand.

IN YOUR OWN LIFE: Based on what you've learned today, what is the next step God is challenging you to take in trusting Him?

DAY 4 FAITH: MARY, MOTHER OF JESUS

"Unwavering trust is a rare and precious thing because it often demands a degree of courage that borders on the heroic."[15]
BRENNAN MANNING

A MATTER OF TRUST

Why is trust important in a marriage?

Why is trust necessary in a parent/child relationship?

Why is it important for church members and their leaders?

Finish the sentence: If there's one person I can trust implicitly, it would be _____.

Put an X where you would place yourself on the scale below:

I trust others easily   I keep my guard up

We may find it hard or easy to trust others, partly depending on our past experiences. Not everyone is trustworthy. But God is. A part of being a faith-filled, legacy-building woman of God is trusting Him implicitly. That means you believe Him not just in the big things but day by day in the small things too. Jesus' mother, Mary, demonstrated this everyday faith just as she showed the mega faith to believe she could conceive the Messiah while still a virgin. This faith showed up when her Son was just starting His ministry. This time, there were no angels or dramatic announcements. It was just another day in Cana, a few miles from Nazareth, at a wedding among friends and neighbors.

IMPLICIT TRUST

Read John 2:1-5. What problem did the bridal couple encounter?

Wedding celebrations in Jesus' day could last up to a week. Families invited the whole town to this extended banquet. It required thoughtful planning to provide enough food and drink for all the guests for the duration of the event. Running out of wine was more than just embarrassing; it violated the strong unwritten social norms of hospitality.[16]

We are not sure how much Mary was responsible for solving the problem, but she saw a way to help. What was her solution?

What do you think Mary expected Jesus to do about the situation?

John described what happened in Cana as Jesus' first miracle (2:11). (Actually John used the word *sign* instead of *miracle*. For John, a sign was more than just an extraordinary event. It was something that pointed to who Jesus really was.) Mary had not yet seen her Son heal the sick, calm the sea, restore sight to the blind, cast out demons, or raise the dead. Yet she knew Him well enough. Tradition holds that her husband, Joseph, was dead by now. Likely she had come to rely on her adult Son in various situations.[17] One thing is clear: She trusted Him implicitly. She believed that by simply telling Him about the problem, He would care and help.

> How do you explain Jesus' seemingly sharp reply to His mother in verse 4?

Jesus was anything but predictable. When you think you know how He'll respond, He always surprises. He frequently responded to those who asked for help by challenging them and testing their faith. When His mom said in essence, "We need a little help here," Jesus basically shot back, "What do you want me to do? It's not my time yet." We need to understand that Jesus was not being harsh to His mother. But neither was He taking orders from her. His mission was to do the will of the Father. As one scholar put it, "Jesus was not being directed by his mother but by a determined hour."[18]

Mary didn't argue with Jesus. But she didn't back down. She probably didn't understand all the implications of His words, but she understood enough to trust His goodness and ability to solve the problem so completely that she could say to the servants without qualification, "Do whatever he tells you" (v. 5).

> Read how Jesus responded to Mary's absolute trust (2:6-10). What surprises or intrigues you about Jesus' first miracle?

UNWAVERING TRUST

The Gospel writers recorded over thirty miracles Jesus performed. People were often helped in the process, but there was a higher purpose. Jesus' miracles demonstrated that He is the Son of God, the Savior of the world. Again, that's why John called them "signs" instead of "miracles." They displayed His glory to nurture people's faith.[19]

> Review verse 11. What significant impact did this miracle have?

Mary herself had already demonstrated her faith in God for the big things when she believed she would give birth as a virgin. She showed faith in Jesus for the everyday things when the wine ran out at a wedding. Trusting God day by day in the big and small things builds an unshakable faith that sustains us in the worst times. So a few years later, when Roman soldiers beat her Son and nailed Him to a cross, Mary had the faith to stay to the end (John 19:25).

In *Trusting God, Even When Life Hurts*, author Jerry Bridges explained it like this:

> *"Trust is not a passive state of mind. It is a vigorous act of the soul by which we choose to lay hold on the promises of God and cling to them despite the adversity that at times seeks to overwhelm us."*[20]

> When have you trusted God for something big and impossible?

What day-to-day things do you trust God for?

When have you held to an unwavering trust in God despite difficult circumstances?

PROVING JESUS OVER AND OVER

Louisa Stead was with her husband and four-year-old daughter, enjoying the beach on Long Island, when they heard the frantic screams of boy who was drowning. Mr. Stead attempted to save him. But the child pulled him under the waves as well and both drowned in front of Louisa and her daughter.[21]

Widowed and without means of support, Louisa landed in extreme poverty. On one particular morning, she had no money or food to get through the day when she opened her front door to find someone had left food and money there. That was the day she wrote "'Tis So Sweet to Trust in Jesus." The chorus is a testimony to her unwavering trust in Jesus' constant faithfulness:

> *"Jesus, Jesus, how I trust Him!*
> *How I've proved Him o'er and o'er!*
> *Jesus, Jesus, precious Jesus!*
> *Oh, for grace to trust Him more!"*[22]

How has God proven to you that you can trust Him implicitly? How have you experienced His faithfulness in your life?

Would you say you're leaving a legacy of faith? Why or why not? What steps do you need to take to do so?

IN YOUR OWN WORDS: Based on what you've studied today, how would you further define faith?

IN YOUR OWN LIFE: Based on what you've learned today, what next step is God challenging you to take in believing Him?

DAY 5 **COURAGE & FAITH**

"Courage is contagious. When a brave man takes a stand, the spines of others are stiffened."[23]

BILLY GRAHAM

Who needs the influence of your courage today? Who needs the influence of your faith?

When Corrie ten Boom and her family were arrested by the German authorities and sent to a concentration camp for sheltering Jews in their home in Holland in 1944, she likely never thought of the influence she would have on so many. In those days, when Corrie and her family defied the Nazis to save Jews by providing a safe hiding place, they had no concept of the multitudes they would impact with their legacy of courage. They simply risked their lives to save those being persecuted because they believed it was the right thing for followers of Christ to do.

Corrie and her sister, Betsie, found themselves in the largest concentration camp for women—Ravensbrück—with a diet of watery soup, a lice-infested bed, and drain holes for toilets. They endured deplorable, dehumanizing conditions by holding onto their faith and sharing it with those around them. The sisters strengthened each other's faith and courage. At one point, Betsie said to Corrie, "[We] must tell people what we have learned here. We must tell them that there is no pit so deep that He is not deeper still. They will listen to us, Corrie, because we have been here."[24] Unfortunately, Corrie saw her sister die at Ravensbrück. She experienced horrors that would drive many people to despair. She struggled with forgiving her captors, yet she never lost her faith in God.

Corrie was freed from the Nazi death camp on December 28, 1944 due to a technical error.[25] Following her release, the Nazis gassed all women in the camp her age and older. Corrie would spend the remaining forty years of her life traveling the world sharing her story at churches, conferences, and in Bible study groups that met in countries where Christians suffer persecution. She could tell people in the worst circumstances that they could trust in God because she knew what He had brought her through. When she died at the age of ninety-one, she had shared her testimony in sixty countries.[26]

Where do you think Corrie learned her faith and courage?

Undoubtedly, Corrie did not plan the life she ended up living. Nor did she likely begin as a young woman deciding, "I want to build a legacy of courage and faith that will impact hundreds of thousands of people."

What decisions do you think she made day by day that allowed her to build a legacy of courage that still impacts people like you and me today?

Read the story of Shadrach, Meshach, and Abednego in Daniel 3, and consider their legacy of faith and courage. How did they display faith? How did they display courage?

What was the legacy of their courage and faith?

You may not be currently facing a crisis like the fiery furnace or Ravensbrück, but what can you do today to begin building your courage and faith for when times of testing do come?

☐ Invest more time in daily prayer
☐ Dedicate time to in-depth Bible study
☐ Trust God with my current problem
☐ Work on cultivating friendships with strong believers who will influence me to have faith and courage
☐ Other:

Commit the following Scripture verse to memory to help you leave a legacy of courage and faith.

> "Haven't I commanded you: be strong and courageous? Do not be afraid or discouraged, for the LORD your God is with you wherever you go."
> **JOSHUA 1:9**
>
> *Deut 31:1-8*

Exodus Process

session two:

BOLDNESS & WITNESS

WATCH

To watch the free video of Session Two, go to LifeWay.com/LegacyStudy.

DISCUSS *Museum in DC*

What is one thing that stood out to you from the video? *Bold to speak brought "Dream Speech"*

How would you define boldness?
*Courage to speak out.
Do right thing when needed.*

When was a time you acted with boldness?

What does it mean to be a witness for Jesus Christ?

If you had an appointment immediately following this group time to share your faith with a friend, how would you feel? Excited? Afraid? Distressed? Explain.

Why is being bold and being a witness so vital to leaving a spiritual legacy?

INTRODUCTION

Bold: "Fearless before danger: Intrepid"[27]
MERRIAM-WEBSTER

Bold: "Not hesitating or fearful in the face of actual or possible danger or rebuff; courageous and daring"[28]
DICTIONARY.COM

Gospel/R&B singer Liz Vice received over one million streams on Spotify for the title track of her first album, "There's a Light." She's appeared on stage with many well-known artists. Audiences mesmerized by her soulful voice would never guess that the accomplished gospel singer ever suffered from stage fright. But she did.

One of five children raised by her mother, Liz remembers waking up every morning as a child to the sound of her mother's voice singing, "Rise and shine and give God the glory." Liz taught herself to play piano, and she performed on her own private "stage" in the family's basement, where she would dance and lip sync songs from the radio and her favorite movie soundtracks.

At just nineteen years of age, Liz encountered serious health problems. She went on kidney dialysis (hemodialysis) for three years and underwent a kidney transplant. This difficult time became a time of healing and gaining perspective. The next year, Liz joined her local church and felt a recurring "nudge" to join the worship team singing background vocals. Despite battling stage fright, she knew "fear could never overpower this unknown 'call.'"[29] She said yes to that call. When Liz sang her first solo, it put her on the path to becoming a gospel singer.

Vice's bio describes her as "very passionate" and having "overcome many obstacles." She attributes her adventurous life in part to her willingness to "being willing and available to wherever it is that the Lord leads. It's all about risk …"[30] Interestingly, when *Christianity Today* magazine asked ten contemporary Christian women to reflect on women in history who influenced their faith in Jesus, Liz Vice named Joan of Arc. Joan of Arc was the teenage girl who claimed to have visions from God, which led her to rally thousands of French troops against the English during the Hundred Years' War. At age eighteen, she was captured, charged with heresy, and burned at the stake. Her last word was "Jesus."[31] Liz explains, "For Joan of Arc to be so young and to lose her *life* for the calling she was so bold and outspoken about—it's amazing."[32]

> What is the boldest thing you've ever done? What inspired you to do it?

DAY 1 **BOLDNESS: WOMEN AT THE WELL**

JESUS MAKES A BOLD CHOICE
Read John 4:1-7.

As Jesus' popularity began to grow, the Pharisees took notice and
watched Him more carefully. Since it was not yet time to reveal who He
was, Jesus moved about to avoid conflict. In this case, it meant leaving
Judea and heading north to Galilee. The most direct route was straight
through Samaria, a journey of three days. For many Jews, however, their
hatred of the Samaritans overrode expediency, and they took the longer
route around Samaria along the Jordan River.

Focus

The Jews' hatred for the Samaritans stemmed back to the days of the
exile. Samaria was strategically situated between Judea and Galilee. Back
when the Assyrians took the Northern Kingdom of Israel captive and
deported many of the Jews, King Sargon of Assyria repopulated Samaria
with exiles from different lands. These foreigners intermarried with the
Jews remaining there. Consequently, their fellow Jews considered them
half-breeds. Jews believed that even associating with Samaritans could
defile them.

Jesus, in His own bold way, cast off concerns for socially acceptable,
politically correct behavior and put Himself in the path of a person
desperately in need of a Savior.

> What word in verse 4 suggests Jesus was intentional
> about His bold choice to go through Samaria instead of
> around it?

John mentions several details leading up to Jesus' encounter with the
Samaritan woman in verses 5-6.

What was said about the time of day, and why do you think it is significant?

Two unusual things happened in verse 7. First, a woman from Sychar came to the well to draw water. Historians have determined there were other wells closer to Sychar than the well of Jacob. It wouldn't make sense for her to walk the greater distance to this well for water unless she had a reason. Plus, she came at noon. This would have been the hottest part of the day, certainly not the time for drawing water. But it was a small town, and she was a woman with a reputation. Encountering the other women of the town there at the local watering hole was likely something she sought to avoid.[33]

Just as unusual was the fact that Jesus, who was both a man and a Jew, spoke to her. Men didn't speak to women in public. And Jews certainly didn't speak to Samaritans.

If you were watching this scene unfold as an unbiased observer, what would you expect to happen next? Why?

A BOLD CONVERSATION
Read John 4:9-15.

The Samaritan woman matched Jesus' boldness with a boldness of her own. Instead of quietly walking away or just giving him a drink wordlessly, she spoke up and questioned Him. Ironically, while speaking to Him, she challenged, "Why are you speaking to me? Don't you know we're not supposed to be speaking to each other?"

This is a good place to talk about what it does and doesn't mean to be bold in the biblical sense. Being bold doesn't mean breaking rules or social conventions just for the sake of being a rule breaker. It's not about being rude or arrogant or obnoxious. It's not about demanding your own way. It's not about having a sense of entitlement.

Rather, biblical boldness is about speaking the truth even when it's unpopular. The bold act without worrying about what other people think or say because they have confidence in following a higher standard. The bold are willing to break with tradition.

Jesus responded to the Samaritan woman's boldness, offering her what He knew she really needed. Unintimidated, the woman engaged in the discussion and met Him word for word. But they were talking on two different levels (vv. 10-15).

What did she think she needed? Water

What did Jesus know she needed? Forgiveness for eternal life.

Jesus was offering her an opportunity to seize life eternal. She was looking to get a lifetime supply of Aquafina™!

When has God challenged you to seize opportunities bigger than what you were grasping for yourself? How did you respond?

Which of the following examples of choosing God's bigger opportunity can you relate to? How does boldness factor into it?

□ Starting a new job or a new position at work
□ Volunteering for a ministry or leadership role
□ Participating in a mission trip
□ Initiating a new relationship or ending a negative relationship
□ Becoming a mother
□ Completing a degree or going back to school
□ Writing a book or starting a blog
□ Speaking in public
□ Mentoring someone
□ Other:

A BOLD INVITATION

Read John 4:16-19.

Notice how masterfully Jesus guided the conversation in verses 16-18. What do you think Jesus intended by bringing up her "husband" and revealing that He knew about her history with men?

This woman had a history. Religious people might say she had no business schmoozing with the Rabbi. They might question why He would invite someone like her to fellowship with Him or drink from the living water. What right did she have?

But of course, none of us has the right. And yet Jesus invites us all to come boldly before the throne of grace and receive mercy because of His sacrifice for us:

"For we do not have a high priest who is unable
to sympathize with our weaknesses, but one who
has been tempted in every way as we are, yet
without sin. Therefore, let us approach the throne
of grace with boldness, so that we may receive
mercy and find grace to help us in time of need."
HEBREWS 4:15-16

Jesus came to be the Savior of the woman who had stumbled through life from husband to husband and now lived with a man she wasn't married to. Over and over she had known rejection and loss. He offered acceptance. He invited her to come boldly and receive the living water of a relationship with Him and learn that only He could satisfy her deepest longing.

He was inviting her to claim with boldness what she did not deserve because He would die to make it her birthright.

If you have trusted Jesus as your Savior, God says these things about you:

- You are My child (Rom. 8:16).

- You are forgiven of your sin (Acts 10:43).

- You are no longer under condemnation (Rom. 8:1).

- You are considered righteous in My sight (Rom. 3:21-26).

- You are filled with (empowered by) the Holy Spirit (Acts 1:8).

- Nothing can separate you from My love (Rom. 8:35-39).

- I will never leave you or forsake you (Heb. 13:5b-6).

- You are a super-conqueror through Me (Rom. 8:37).

How does knowing these things give you boldness to speak out, take a stand for truth, or take the next step of obedience in your situation?

In the list of things God says about you, underline the statement that gives you the most confidence to follow Him boldly without concern for what others think. Explain your choice in the space provided.

Sometimes it can be difficult to connect truths in God's Word from our heads to our hearts. How can you grow in your belief of what God says about you?

BOLDLY SEEKING MORE
Read John 4:19-27.

Her sad, sinful life exposed, the Samaritan woman tried to deflect the conversation yet remained and continued to talk to Jesus. She didn't back down or run away. She wanted to know more. She started grilling the Rabbi about a theological point of controversy between the Samaritans and the Jews. Her bold questioning and discussion of the coming Messiah left Jesus the perfect opening to reveal to her that He was the Messiah she sought.

How bold are you in seeking to know and understand Jesus more? (Circle a number along the spectrum that reflects where you are.)

1   2   3   4   5   6   7   8   9   10
Really rather timid   Pursuing Him relentlessly

Explain your answer:

How did the disciples react to the boldness of Jesus and the Samaritan woman (v. 27)?

Jesus continually amazed people with His boldness. He did things no one else would attempt to do and said things nobody else dared say.

What is God calling you to boldly do or say that would amaze the people around you?

IN YOUR OWN WORDS: Based on what you've studied today, how would you define boldness?

IN YOUR OWN LIFE: Based on what you've learned today, what is the next step God is challenging you to take toward building a legacy of boldness?

DAY 2 BOLDNESS: WOMAN AT THE WELL

"People pay attention when they see that God actually changes persons and sets them free. When a new Christian stands up and tells how God has revolutionized his or her life, no one dozes off."[34]
JIM CYMBALA

A FEW BRAVE MEN ... AND WOMEN
Who is a woman you admire for her boldness? Why?

In yesterday's lesson, we talked about some things boldness is and isn't. For a quick review, underline the phrases that represent what boldness *is*. Cross through the phrases that represent what boldness is *not*.

☐ Taking risks to follow God's leading
☐ Not worrying about what other people think
☐ Being arrogant
☐ Being rude
☐ Pursuing more of God
☐ Being unafraid to challenge the status quo
☐ Doing what's right regardless of what others do
☐ Speaking up
☐ Standing your ground
☐ Looking out for number one
☐ Trusting in yourself
☐ Trusting in God

We're talking about the bold who passionately pursue more of God in their lives. Think Jacob wrestling with God and telling Him, "I will not let you go unless you bless me" (Gen. 32:26). Think Paul, who considered "everything to be loss in view of the surpassing value of knowing Christ Jesus" (Phil. 3:8).

We're talking about the bold who do what is right regardless of others' opinions. Think Peter and John, who answered the Jewish authorities who had arrested them for preaching the gospel, "Whether it's right in the sight of God for us to listen to you rather than to God, you decide; for we are unable to stop speaking about what we have seen and heard" (Acts 4:19-20). Think of the woman who lovingly anointed Jesus with expensive perfume even though Jesus' own disciples criticized her (Matt. 26:6-13).

We're talking about the bold who take risks to follow where God leads when the path is unclear. Think Abram leaving his home and people to follow God's call, not knowing where it would lead (Gen. 12:1-4). Think of the twelve disciples, who left everything to follow Jesus simply because He said, "Follow me" (Luke 5:1-11).

And think of the Samaritan woman at the well. Yesterday we saw how she responded to Jesus' bold move to speak to her and request a drink of water. She engaged with a boldness of her own. Undeterred by what was considered appropriate or what anyone might think, she carried on an extended conversation with this man, this Jew she did not know. When Jesus hinted He could provide an endless supply of water, she boldly asked for some. Then we saw Jesus respond to the woman's fearless determination by revealing that He was the Messiah she was looking for.

SHE FOUND HER VOICE

Read John 4:28-30.

What's one item you almost never leave home without? Why? What might cause you to leave it?

What did the Samaritan woman leave behind (v. 28)? It's not like she could pick up another one at the store close to her house. Why do you think she left it?

She came to the well to draw physical water. But instead she heard about living water in a transformative conversation with Jesus. Once her life was changed, drawing water plunged down the priority list. She now had a new mission—to tell others about Jesus. Leaving the water jar was representative of her thirst for true life, of her walking in the new life she found in the Messiah.

As we noted yesterday, her scandalous lifestyle gave the Samaritan woman every reason to avoid her neighbors. But now we see her running into town unashamedly.

What made the difference? What do you think gave her the boldness to share what she had discovered regardless of how people might feel about her or whether they might believe her?

Had anything changed in their perception of her? How do you think she expected them to receive her and her message?

There is something about being in the presence of Jesus. Seeing Him as He really is puts our problems in perspective and makes our enemies appear weak. Remember the song, "Turn Your Eyes Upon Jesus"?

> "Turn your eyes upon Jesus,
> Look full in His wonderful face,
> And the things of earth will grow strangely dim
> In the light of His glory and grace."[35]

Go back to that earlier reference about Peter and John telling the Jewish authorities who arrested them they couldn't stop preaching Jesus (Acts 4:19–20). Do you know what the authorities, who were Peter and John's adversaries, determined about the two men?

> "When they observed the boldness of Peter and
> John and realized that they were uneducated
> and untrained men, they were amazed and
> recognized that they had been with Jesus."
> **ACTS 4:13**

Being with Jesus transformed those common, uneducated fishermen into passionate, bold, articulate communicators.

One encounter with Jesus changed the Samaritan woman from a recluse ashamed of her life to a passionate evangelist running to tell about the man who had told her "everything I ever did" (John 4:39). Life transformation had taken place.

When has time with Jesus changed your perspective on a problem or situation and given you new boldness?

PEOPLE PAY ATTENTION WHEN GOD CHANGES A PERSON
Read John 4:39-42.

Look back at verses 29-30. Do you think the townspeople were immediately convinced by the Samaritan woman's testimony that Jesus was the Messiah? What did her message convince them to do?

The woman did not have the most trustworthy reputation. But people saw something different in her that convinced them to check out this man she was raving about.

What was the result of the Samaritan woman's boldness? What was her legacy in that town? How did her decision to believe in Jesus change her legacy?

Read John 4:31-38.

These verses tell what was happening with Jesus and His disciples while the Samaritan woman ran back to tell her neighbors about Jesus. The disciples were worried about getting Jesus something to eat. He basically told them He was more concerned with doing His Father's work than with fish and chips. He pointed them to the harvest for eternal life He came to earth for. That was His priority. So missing lunch to bring this Samaritan woman eternal life was not a problem. Jesus saw the harvest her faith would yield. Not only would she believe, but she would lead her neighbors to find Jesus.

In fact, this large conversion of Samaritans starting in Sychar marked the beginning of the universal scope of Jesus' saving mission. It would continue to grow as the gospel spread to the Gentiles through the mission of the early church.[36] So you see, the legacy of the Samaritan woman's bold faith continued to send ripples beyond what anyone, except Jesus, might have imagined. Your bold faith in response to Jesus can do the same.

IN YOUR OWN WORDS: Based on what you've studied today, what would you say makes a legacy of boldness?

IN YOUR OWN LIFE: What evidence is there that you are currently building a legacy of boldness? What changes need to take place for you to do so?

DAY 3 WITNESS: MARY MAGDALENE

"Evangelism is witness. It is one beggar telling another beggar where to get food."[37]

D. T. NILES

In yesterday's lesson, the Samaritan woman met the Man who told her everything she had ever done. Believing Him to be the Messiah, she ran and told the people of her town. The joy of her discovery gave her a newfound boldness to go and tell the good news. We saw how there is something about the transforming power of Jesus Christ that compels us to want to share Him with others. And His Spirit can replace our fear with a boldness to speak for Him.

MARY WHO?

Read John 20:1-10.

As was characteristic of John as a writer, he used Mary Magdalene to represent a type of person—in this case, the group of women who went to Jesus' tomb early after the Sabbath to anoint the body with spices (Mark 16:1; Matt. 28:1; Luke 24:10). Notice the "we" Mary used in John 20:2.

List everything else you discover about Mary Magdalene from the following passages: Luke 8:1-3; John 19:25; Matthew 27:45-61; Mark 15:40-41,45-47.

What did Mary assume when she saw the empty tomb? Why do you think that was her conclusion?

Read John 20:11-18. What verb in verse 11 tells us Mary's response to finding Jesus' body gone? What does that response say about her state of mind?

This was no polite sniffle; it was a big, ugly cry. The Greek word John used was the term associated with anguished crying or wailing by mourners at funerals and during times of bereavement. Think loud and unrestrained bawling.

When was Mary's *aha* moment, when she recognized that Jesus was alive and everything in her world had changed?

Do you remember the moment your eyes were opened to the truth that Jesus is the Son of God and your personal Savior? Explain.

What was Mary's natural inclination when she realized Jesus was alive and she had not lost Him after all? What did Jesus direct her to do instead?

A RELIABLE WITNESS?

If we had arranged Jesus' first resurrection appearance, it probably would have been before the Jewish and Roman authorities who had ordered Him to be crucified—the men in seats of power. It would have been a big "I told you so." And throughout history it would forever silence Jesus' critics because the people who said He wasn't the Son of God would have to admit He was. Instead, Jesus quietly showed Himself to someone who already believed in Him, a woman at that. And not just any woman, but that woman who had trouble with demons. Who would believe her? Why should they? And why would Jesus choose her? But then again, why does God do a lot of things the way He does?

Paul gives us a clue in 1 Corinthians 1:26-29:

> "Brothers and sisters, consider your calling: Not many were wise from a human perspective, not many powerful, not many of noble birth. Instead, God has chosen what is foolish in the world to shame the wise, and God has chosen the weak in the world to shame the strong. God has chosen what is insignificant and despised in the world—what is viewed as nothing— to bring to nothing what is viewed as something, so that no one may boast in His presence."

God could publish His message of salvation to the world any number of ways that might be much more efficient and polished than using people like us. He doesn't need us to get His work done. He is God. But He chooses to use us. Not because of our great communication skills or impressive Bible knowledge, and not because we're adept at convincing people. No, He chooses us despite ourselves! Because through our weakness He can show His power and glory.

How can God show His power through your weakness when you share about Him?

Christian apologist, theologian, and philosopher William Lane Craig explains how the "weakness" of the testimony of Mary and the other women at the tomb actually corroborates the veracity of the resurrection as a historical event rather than a mere legend:

> "If the empty tomb story were a legend, then it is most likely that the male disciples would have been made to be the first to discover the empty tomb. The fact that women, whose testimony was deemed worthless, were the chief witnesses to the fact of the empty tomb can only be plausibly explained if, like it or not, they actually were the discoverers of the empty tomb. Hence, the gospels are most likely giving an accurate account of this matter."[38]

A STORY ONLY YOU CAN TELL

Based on her life experience and relationship with Jesus, what did Mary Magdalene have to share that nobody else did?

John was "the one Jesus loved" (John 20:2). Peter had walked on water with Jesus. Thomas would be able to say he had seen Jesus' wounds up close. But only Mary could say, "I was the first to see Jesus after His resurrection. He called me by name. I know He is alive because He met me in the garden."

Luke identified Mary Magdalene among a group of women who traveled with Jesus and His disciples (Luke 8:1-3). These women had been healed of sicknesses and evil spirits, and they supported Jesus' ministry with their resources. They were women of means. Luke called out Mary specifically for having been healed of seven demons. Jewish historian J. Klausner described her as "a woman who had suffered from hysterics to the verge of madness."[39] We may not know the exact nature or extent of what Luke referred to as her "seven demons," but we can appreciate that Jesus had freed her from something that had a horrible grip on her life. He had dramatically and permanently changed her life.

In a short paragraph, write your story of how Jesus has changed your life.

Reread verse 18. What was Mary's response to Jesus' instructions?

Check out the response Mary received to her witness in Mark 16:9-11.

What does Mary's example teach you about what it means to be a "successful" witness for Jesus?

We need to keep in mind that not all who hear the good news of the gospel will believe it. But their possible rejection of the message does not negate our calling and our responsibility to tell it. We, like Mary, must continue to joyfully bear witness to the hope and grace found only in Jesus Christ.

IN YOUR OWN WORDS: Based on what you've studied today, how would you define witnessing?

IN YOUR OWN LIFE: What is the next step God is challenging you to take toward building a legacy of witness?

*"Be brave enough to start a
conversation that matters."*[40]
MARGARET WHEATLEY

A MODEL WITNESS

Recently, in a Bible study about friendship, we were discussing our attitude toward friends. The leader said, "I don't know about you all, but I go hard after my friends." She meant she's intentional about cultivating friendships. She invests time with friends. She initiates invitations to get together. She keeps in touch. She's there for her friends when they need her. She remembers their birthdays and anniversaries. She goes out of her way to nurture those relationships.

What in your life do you "go hard after"?

In 1999, Rebecca Manley Pippert authored a classic book on witnessing called *Out of the Saltshaker & into the World: Evangelism as a Way of Life.* She wrote:

> "If you live by the same values and priorities [Jesus] had, you will find evangelism happening naturally. It becomes a lifestyle and not a project."[41]

Jesus illustrated His values succinctly in the parable of the lost sheep (Luke 15:1-7). The Pharisees had criticized Jesus for mingling with sinners. Jesus explained His priorities with a story about a shepherd who owns a hundred sheep. When just one sheep wanders off and gets lost, the shepherd leaves the ninety-nine in pursuit of the one and keeps searching until he finds it. In other words, he goes hard after the lost.

That's exactly what Philip did in Acts 8, which is why he became the kind of Christ follower who left a legacy of witness that extended far beyond his lifetime. Just like Mary Magdalene, he is a model for us to follow today in what it means to be a witness for Jesus Christ.

Philip was one of the seven men chosen by the early church to distribute charity to the Hellenistic widows. He qualified for selection because he was "full of the Spirit and wisdom" (Acts 6:3). When persecution broke out against the church in Jerusalem and its members fled in all directions, Philip went north to a city in Samaria (8:4-5).

What do you recall from Session Two, Day 1 about how Jews viewed Samaritans?

It seems Philip, following the example of Christ (John 4), moved beyond the long-held Jewish prejudice and began preaching the gospel to the Samaritans. God also empowered him to do miraculous signs among them. And many believed. Because His ministry there was going so well, word of it got back to the church in Jerusalem. They then sent Peter and John to check out what was going on in Samaria (8:14,25). Peter and John joined Philip in his ministry there briefly, and when they left, they also preached in Samaritan cities on their way back to Jerusalem. In other words, Philip was in the middle of a thriving ministry, making a huge impact. So there could be no possible reason to stop what he was doing and do something else, right? Wrong!

LIFE INTERRUPTED

Read Acts 8:26-29.

God sent an angel to interrupt Philip's thriving ministry and send him to an unlikely place. The road to Gaza was the last watering place before the desert on the way to Egypt.[42]

What was Philip's response to being interrupted? Does it surprise you? Why or why not?

Describe a time when you came to realize that something you had regarded as an inconvenient interruption was actually a divine appointment?

Philip's divine appointment was waiting for him on the road to Gaza.

Review verses 26-28 and list all that you discover about the person Philip encountered.

Notice the direction Philip received from the Holy Spirit next (v. 29).

Considering your current disposition for talking with strangers about Jesus, how do you think you might have responded in this situation?

CHASE YOUR CHARIOTS

Read Acts 8:30-35. Find the verb in verse 30 that tells how Philip got to the chariot and write it here:

That's right. Philip chased down the chariot. He didn't wake up that morning and think, *I'm going to find and chase down a man in a chariot today.* But he was sensitive to the Holy Spirit's leading and willing to follow. Philip allowed God's priorities to become his priorities. So when God determined it was time for an encounter with a certain Ethiopian man in a chariot on the road to Gaza, Philip ran to join in that encounter at that precise window of opportunity.

Rebecca Manley Pippert wrote,

"Jesus ... wants us to see that the neighbor next door or the people sitting next to us on a plane or in a classroom are not interruptions to our schedule. They are there by divine appointment. Jesus wants us to see their needs, their loneliness, their longings, and he wants to give us the courage to reach out to them."[43]

Take a moment to ask God to help you see the people He has divinely placed in your life for you to reach out to with the hope of the gospel.

Identify one person God has placed in your path to hear your witness of Christ. How can you run hard after that person?

How did Philip interact with the Ethiopian man in a way that made the man feel open to hearing Philip rather than defensive and closed down?

Philip followed the leading of the Spirit and approached the man. But notice he didn't immediately jump up in the chariot and forcefully state, "Hey, brother! You're lost and need to get saved!" No, he simply met the man where he was. Philip observed, asked a question, then shared the Scripture.

How can you translate Philip's actions into your current opportunities to share Christ with others?

SEIZING YOUR DIVINE ENCOUNTER MOMENT
Read Acts 8:36-39.

Philip allowed himself to become God's mouthpiece to an Ethiopian man in a chariot on the road to Gaza during a brief window of time on a specific day. Because Philip made himself available, God did what only He can do in convicting that man and calling him to repentance. You might say, "Sure, that's easy for someone like Philip. Preaching and witnessing were second nature to him."

Read what Rebecca Manley Pippert adds to the conversation:

"Being an extrovert isn't essential to evangelism—obedience and love are."[44]

And this:

"When God is seeking a person, he will not allow my fear, my feeling of intimidation or my lack of knowledge or experience to prevent that person from finding him."[45]

Remember the woman at the well? God used her witness despite, and perhaps even because of, her inadequacies. He shows His power best through our weakness. God uses people who make themselves available to Him.

In Philip's life journey, his path intersected with the Ethiopian man's for only a short time.

Sometimes, we have only a brief window of opportunity for a divine encounter that could change someone's eternity. That's what happened for Philip and the Ethiopian. But we have to recognize that the impact of Philip's witness didn't stop with that one man. This Ethiopian official would return home, where he would potentially bear witness to his coworkers and neighbors.

At that time, Greeks and Romans considered Ethiopia the extreme outer boundary of the civilized world.[46] In this way, Philip's witness fulfilled Christ's commission to take the gospel to Jerusalem, Judea, Samaria, and the ends of the earth (Acts 1:8). Because Philip obeyed the Holy Spirit's nudge to go to the desert road leading to Gaza and then to chase the man in the chariot and speak to him about Jesus, the gospel made its way to the ends of the earth.

In the same way, you may never know the impact you can make by simply sharing the gospel with one person. God could use your obedient witness to make a difference in nations and generations.

NEXT STEPS

Check out these practical online resources to help you share your faith. In the space provided, write down some tips you can put into practice from the articles.

https://billygraham.org/story/sharing-your-faith-101/

https://www.christianitytoday.com/biblestudies/articles/evangelism/051012.html

http://www.lifeway.com/en/articles/everyday-evangelism

IN YOUR OWN WORDS: Based on what you've studied today, how would you further define what it means to witness?

IN YOUR OWN LIFE: Based on what you've learned today, what is the next step God is challenging you to take toward building a legacy of witness?

DAY 5 **BOLDNESS & WITNESS**

"Boldness is acting, by the power of the Holy Spirit, on an urgent conviction in the face of some threat. ... If we can now 'with confidence draw near to the throne of grace' ... who then should we fear ...? Jesus did not die on the cross to have us quivering in a corner because some human being might say something mean, or stop our paychecks, or sever a relationship, or even kill us."[47]
JON BLOOM

WE DON'T LIKE TO BE UNPOPULAR

When pastor and author Francis Chan stood before tens of thousands to speak at Together 2016 on the National Mall in Washington, D.C., he stated, "I'm just noticing that there are very few people who are spreading the gospel, and I think I know why."[48] He observed that Christians are willing to give ourselves to good, social causes like caring for the poor, fighting human trafficking, and standing for racial reconciliation, as well we should. But, he challenged, we often compromise the gospel while hiding behind these good causes. That's because it is politically correct to work for social justice and fight for the disenfranchised. Conversely, certain points of the gospel message are not politically correct at all: We are all sinners under judgment for our sin; the penalty is death and hell; Jesus is the only way of salvation.[49] To state these truths unequivocally is pretty bold, and it can make you unpopular. We don't like to be unpopular. But it seems to have gone beyond a popularity issue. A 2019 Barna study showed that half of millennial evangelicals say it's wrong to evangelize.[50]

Chan quoted the passage from Matthew 10, where Jesus told His disciples He was sending them out like sheep among wolves. Jesus said they would be delivered over to the courts, beaten in the synagogues, and dragged before governors and kings for His sake to bear witness (vv. 17-18). "I think the biggest challenge in this generation is what we just read," Chan commented. "In a generation that is obsessed with popularity and being liked and getting 'Likes,' Jesus says the way to become significant and to have an impact is through rejection."[51]

Would you agree? Do you find it easier to take a stand for a social issue or share the gospel message, knowing your audience could find it offensive? Explain.

Read John 15:18-25. What should you expect if you follow Jesus and obey His command to tell others about Him?

Nobody likes rejection. And having the boldness to do what you know you should without concern over whether people will reject you for it … well, that doesn't come naturally to most people.

SEEKING BOLDNESS
Notice what Peter and John and their fellow believers prayed after the two disciples were arrested and threatened for preaching about Jesus.

Read Acts 4:29. What did they pray for?

Now read Acts 4:31. What was the result?

Paul wrote his letter to the Ephesians while he was imprisoned (Eph. 3:1; 4:1).

Considering these circumstances, what would have been a logical prayer request from Paul?

Read Ephesians 6:19-20. What was his actual prayer request to the Ephesians?

It's interesting to note that Peter, John, and Paul, who were incredibly bold for Christ, still felt they needed God's help to keep acting with boldness. They were still dependent on Him to give them the boldness to stand up for Him in whatever situation they would face next. You, too, can ask for boldness. Make it a part of your daily prayer.

A LEGACY OF BOLDNESS AND WITNESS

Read Philippians 1:12-14. What happened to Paul as a result of his publicly speaking about Jesus?

What happened to other believers because of Paul's boldness and resulting imprisonment?

How can your boldness and witness for Christ impact others?

What are the most significant things you learned in this week of study?

What changes will you make to leave a legacy of boldness and witness?

Commit this verse to memory to help you leave behind a legacy of boldness and witness:

"For I am not ashamed of the gospel, because it is the power of God for salvation to everyone who believes, first to the Jew, and also to the Greek."
ROMANS 1:16

session three:

COMPASSION & RESCUE

LEGACY

WATCH

To watch the free video of Session Three, go to LifeWay.com/LegacyStudy.

DISCUSS

What is one thing that stood out to you from the video?

Does "calling" only apply to ministers? Explain.

Lauren stated, "Calling is discovered as God writes consistent themes on our hearts." What does that mean and do you agree? Why or why not?

How would you define compassion?

Would you say that you are a compassionate person? Why or why not?

How do compassion and rescue go hand in hand?

INTRODUCTION

"It may take place in a foreign land or it may take place in your backyard, but I believe that we were each created to change the world for someone."[52]
KATIE DAVIS

Like most of her peers, Katie Davis graduated from high school with a diploma in one hand and a fistful of big dreams in the other. But she did not hold fast to the hopes of a university; she wanted Uganda.

As a senior, Katie wanted to visit an orphanage she had found online; her parents agreed, so in December of 2006 she traveled more than seven thousand miles away from home. In Uganda, she met Pastor Isaac Wagaba and got a glimpse into her future as he laid on the table an offer for her to teach kindergarten at his orphanage.

Not long after graduation Katie got on a plane to Africa. She arrived and immediately started doing what she does best: loving children. As a kindergarten teacher, she invested in her students. With hugs, songs, games, and laughter, she found ways to connect with them.

While walking students home from school, she noticed many children begging, sitting idle, and working in the fields. She discovered that there were only a small number of government-run public schools in Uganda, and none near her area. Private schools were far more common, but the extreme poverty that plagued her new surroundings made that option impossible. Enter divine inspiration.

God gave Katie the idea for a way to meet the needs of the children—a sponsorship program. Within months, Amazima International Ministries (*Amazima* means "truth" in the local language, Luganda) was up and running. The original goal was to get sponsors for forty children. By January 2008, Katie had 150 children signed up to attend school. The ministry provided school supplies, basic medical care, and two hot meals a day.

But Katie's purpose in Uganda didn't end with Amazima. Life changed dramatically for her, when, one day, tragedy struck three young girls in her circle of students. Their parents were dead, and they were living in a hut by themselves, the eldest caring for the other two. One of the hut walls collapsed on the oldest child, and at the hospital Katie overheard the doctors and police discussing not treating the girl because she had no guardian and no money to pay. Katie intervened. Before the day was done, custody papers for all three girls were in her hands. She had quickly gone from being Auntie Katie to Mommy.

She started with three daughters, and the number increased. Every day. Children from the villages, covered in red dirt, stopped at her house on the way to and from school for showers, for food, for a tickle fight, or for a hug. By the time she was twenty-three, she had thirteen daughters. Under Katie's roof the hungry, sick, lonely, and needy found shelter.

"People tell me I am brave. People tell me I am strong. People tell me good job," says Katie. "Well here is the truth of it: I am really not that brave, I am not really that strong, and I am not doing anything spectacular. I am just doing what God called me to do as a follower of Him. Feed His sheep, do unto the least of His people."[53]

More than a decade after she hopped on a plane to Africa, Katie, her husband Benji, and their now fifteen children continue to live out God's call to compassion and rescue in Uganda.

What is your response to Katie's story? Are you willing to take similar action? Explain.

DAY 1 **COMPASSION:**

PHARAOH'S DAUGHTER

From childhood, many of us have heard and loved the Bible story of baby Moses hidden from Pharaoh's murderous plan, safely floating in the water in a basket made by his mother. In today's study, we will focus our attention on Pharaoh's daughter, who played an important role in Moses' story because of her compassionate actions.

The story unfolds against the much bigger backdrop of the generations of people of Israel who had lived and labored as slaves in Egypt. As the Israelites increased in number, Pharaoh, who ruled the land of Egypt, grew increasingly worried about their potential power. So he issued a death decree commanding that all boys born to the people of Israel were to be thrown into the Nile River to die (Ex. 1:22).

Read Exodus 2:1-6.

Following the evil decree, Moses' mother, who was obviously a resourceful woman, constructed a rescue plan for Moses in the form of a waterproof basket. And so it was that baby Moses, about three months old, was floating in a basket among the reeds at the edge of the Nile while his sister, Miriam, stood watch nearby.

Then Pharaoh's daughter entered the scene, arriving with her servant girls to bathe in the Nile River. Spotting the basket in the water, she sent a servant girl to retrieve it. Pharaoh's daughter's plans—a visit to the Nile for bathing—were briefly interrupted while she stopped to investigate the basket in the water.

"WHAT NOW?"
Interruptions pop up all day as we go through the habits and patterns of our lives.

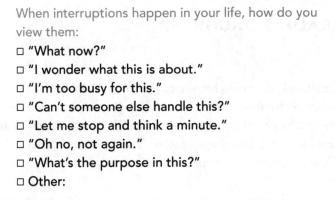

When interruptions happen in your life, how do you view them:
- ☐ "What now?"
- ☐ "I wonder what this is about."
- ☐ "I'm too busy for this."
- ☐ "Can't someone else handle this?"
- ☐ "Let me stop and think a minute."
- ☐ "Oh no, not again."
- ☐ "What's the purpose in this?"
- ☐ Other:

Perhaps she was simply curious, but Pharaoh's daughter paused for a closer look when something unexpected interrupted her day. She saw that the basket cradled a baby boy, and she realized it was one of the "Hebrew boys" (v. 6). The baby was crying.

What does verse 6 tell us was Pharaoh's daughter's reaction when she saw the crying baby?

Note how some of the different Bible translations describe the way Pharaoh's daughter reacted when she saw the baby for the first time:

- "she felt sorry for him" (CSB)

- "she took pity on him" (AMP)

- "she had compassion on him" (NKJV)

- "her heart went out to him" (MSG)

The Holman Illustrated Bible Dictionary's definition of "compassion" is "to enter sympathetically into one's sorrow and pain."[54] There are at least five different Hebrew words used for *compassion* in the Old Testament.

In this story of Pharaoh's daughter, the word used in Exodus 2:6 is *chamal*, which means "to regret," "to be sorry for (to pity)," "to grieve over," or "to spare someone."[55]

When has someone showed compassion toward you?

What impact did that person's compassion have on you?

Being a person who looks for ways, big and small, to demonstrate compassion toward others can have a lasting impact on his or her home and community. By cultivating a legacy of compassion, a person touches others' lives in tangible, significant ways.

COMPASSION VS. SYMPATHY VS. EMPATHY

Compassion, sympathy, and *empathy* are three words that we use—sometimes interchangeably—when we talk about feeling other people's suffering and pain.

Consider how these three words have similar meanings. Then think about how they are different. Write your own definition for each of the words below:

Compassion means:

Sympathy means:

Empathy means:

Maybe you want to look up the words in a dictionary and see how your definitions line up with the dictionary definitions. All three words are related to the idea of seeing and understanding what another person is feeling. But with compassion, there is the added next step of acting to relieve the pain a person is experiencing. A person who develops a legacy of compassion sees and takes action to help meet the needs of others. A compassionate person acts.

Read Exodus 2:7-10.

Note that Pharaoh's daughter saw the baby and felt sorry for him—then she acted with a plan to care for the baby.

Why is action a necessary part of compassion?

What was the result of Pharaoh's daughter's compassion?

Some might look at the events described in Exodus 2 and think, *How lucky, the baby ends up cared for by his mother after all!* But when God is part of the story, there is no luck, and there are no coincidences. God is in the details. He worked in the details of Moses' life, and He works in the details of our lives today.

How is Pharaoh's daughter's finding Moses another example of God's divine appointments—not just a coincidence?

What was the long-term impact of her simple act of compassion in saving the baby?

When have you observed God's far-reaching plans at work in your own life?

We need to be aware that the seemingly random coincidences popping up during the course of our days might actually be divine appointments in which God is giving us the opportunity to see and to act with compassion. Look at these divine appointments as God-given opportunities for you to grow your legacy of compassion.

Compassion is not a one-time good deed where we check off the compassion box as "done." Like physical exercise, it requires focused attention and discipline. Cultivating compassion is a daily commitment of seeing and acting as we encounter needs or pain we can ease.

Maybe you struggle with trying to know where and how to help others in need. In light of so much suffering in the world, how do you know where to get involved?

RISKY BUSINESS

Sometimes when we act with compassion to help someone who needs a hand we have to take risks. Compassion might mean risking some of our resources, our time, our relationships, or our energy.

In what ways did Pharaoh's daughter take risks in acting with compassion?

Building a legacy of compassion will require you to take risks. Compassion will cost you your comfort. But the long-reaching benefits are worth the risk for those who feel the warm touch of your compassion.

IN YOUR OWN WORDS: Reflecting on the story of Pharaoh's daughter and her care for Moses, how would you define compassion?

IN YOUR OWN LIFE: What choices could you make in the days ahead toward building a legacy of compassion?

DAY 2 **COMPASSION: JESUS**

Are there times when you struggle to be compassionate? Likely each of us can recall a time when our compassion was buried down deep inside us and never made it to the surface in our words or actions.

In today's study, let's look for ways to cultivate greater compassion for those God has placed in our lives.

Across the pages of the Old and New Testaments, we find stories of people who acted with great compassion. Their actions stand as a model and inspiration to us, showing us what compassion lived out looks like.

In the Gospels, we see compassion at work over and over again in the life of Jesus, as He encountered people during His three-year ministry. We find one such example in Luke 7.

A MOTHER MOURNS
Read Luke 7:11-12.

Like other widows during Bible times, this woman was both defenseless and unprotected. In the ancient world, men afforded women the financial support and physical protection they needed. Women of that time usually lacked the freedoms, abilities, or training to go out into the world and earn money to provide for themselves. The widow described in Luke 7 was burying her only son when she encountered Jesus. The future looked bleak for her. With no husband or son, she was likely headed toward a life of begging, slavery, or total dependence on others.

What feelings might the woman have had on that day, before her encounter with Jesus?

When have you experienced similar feelings?

THEN EVERYTHING CHANGED

Jesus arrived in Nain, a village in southwest Galilee, at the moment a funeral procession for the son of the widow was passing through the town. There was a large crowd present—Jesus' disciples, other people following Him, the funeral procession—to witness the events that unfolded.

> Read Luke 7:13-17. What was Jesus' initial reaction when He saw the woman? What were His actions?

Jesus responded with compassion in both word and deed.

The widow's son was not in a closed coffin; he was on a bier, which is like a stretcher that was used to carry the body to its burial place.[56] It's also important to know that anyone who touched a corpse became ceremonially unclean for seven days (Num. 19:11). The person who was unclean was required to make a sin offering in order to be purified. If a person failed to carry out the required cleansings, they could be banished from the community (Num. 19:13). So Jesus took a risk when He stopped to engage with this grieving widow and to heal her son.

How might risk be involved in order to show compassion to another person?

This encounter with Jesus changed everything for the woman. She regained her son. Looking ahead, she likely regained some financial safety and protection in her community. She went from being a grieving widow with no resources to a mother with a son and a beautiful story to tell of Jesus' compassion. Her life changed drastically because she met Jesus on what looked like the worst day of her life.

When have you seen one person's compassion change the lives of others?

COMPASSIONATE ACTION

This story in Luke 7 of Jesus showing compassion to the widow is just one of many New Testament stories where His compassion was on display. Search a few more of the following stories to see Jesus acting with compassion.

Fill in the blanks below, describing what Jesus did when He felt compassion for people:

1. Matthew 9:35-38—Jesus "felt compassion" and He
_____.
2. Matthew 15:29-39—Jesus had "compassion on the crowd" and He _____.
3. Mark 1:40-45—Jesus was "moved with compassion" and He _____.
4. Mark 6:30-34—Jesus "had compassion on them" and He _____.

With Jesus, action always accompanied compassion. When we see hurting people, we also must move to action.

How do we practice the same kind of compassion that Jesus showed?

First, let's make it a habit to remember the compassion that has been shown to us.

Lamentations 3:22-23 (AMP) says,

> "It is because of the Lᴏʀᴅ's lovingkindnesses
> that we are not consumed,
> Because His [tender] compassions never fail.
> They are new every morning;
> Great and beyond measure is Your faithfulness!"

How might it shape your day if you woke up each morning reminding yourself of God's compassion toward you that is "new every morning"?

Reminding ourselves of God's abundant compassion toward us can encourage our hearts to show compassion to others. Recalling God's compassion during the seasons of our lives when we have experienced hurt and discouragement allows us to be generous with our compassion for those around us who are hurting right now.

Also, to show the compassion of Jesus we must see people as He did and have hearts sensitive to their needs. Because Christ lives in us through the presence of the Spirit, we have the supernatural ability to do so. But we must be submitted to His lordship and leadership. Without that, we can easily become blinded by our own needs and agendas.

And then, when we do see those in need, we must act. Although we can't raise the dead, we do have the opportunity, calling, and ability to minister to people in need in a myriad of ways. Remember, compassion without action is not really compassion at all.

> **IN YOUR OWN WORDS:** How could cultivating a legacy of compassion change the atmosphere in your home? In your work? At your church? On social media?

> **IN YOUR OWN LIFE:** Following Jesus' example, where are you willing to take some risks to show compassion to someone who needs your help?

DAY 3 RESCUE: JEHOSHEBA

In a world swimming with needs, we may wonder what we can to do rescue people who are suffering in some way.

What can one person do? Plenty, if you look at Oral Lee Brown's life.

Oral Lee Brown stopped at the grocery store one morning in 1987 to pick up a few items. A young girl walked up and asked Brown for a quarter. All Brown had was a $5 bill, so she asked the girl to come into the store with her, and there she told the girl to pick out whatever she wanted. Thinking the child might choose candy or gum, Brown was surprised when she chose to buy a loaf of bread. When Brown asked the girl if she went to school, her reply was "Sometimes."[57]

Following that encounter, Brown had a restless night and could not sleep. She decided she had to find that little girl. Brown visited the school the girl likely attended, but she was never able to reconnect with the child. But at that school, she did find many other children who were struggling in difficult conditions. Wanting to do something to help the children, Brown "adopted" a class of twenty-three first graders in East Oakland, California. She promised them, "Stay in school, and I'll send you to college."[58]

To back up her promise, Brown, who is a real estate agent, began saving $10,000 each year from her $45,000 salary. Besides saving her money, Brown also invested her time in the lives of the children, making regular visits to the classroom, tutoring the students on Saturdays, and meeting with their parents. Brown kept track of the children's attendance and their grades. During the year she provided school supplies, and at Christmas she brought them gifts. As the children got older she took them to visit colleges, and at the end of their senior year Brown attended nine different high school graduation ceremonies. From that class of twenty-three first graders, nineteen students enrolled in college, and three other students attended trade schools. All those students graduated from college in 2003 and 2004.

"I feel the students must be given the financial assistance and inspiration to continue their education" Brown says. "If these children become successful, then my life will have been a success. After this, I will look forward to helping others."[59]

Since that first class, Brown has adopted more students—a total of 136 students have been blessed through her generosity. Brown has also established the Oral Lee Brown Foundation, a non-profit corporation that provides "education assistance and scholarships to underprivileged children in the Oakland area."[60]

Oral Lee Brown has rescued these children, providing a path to college and job training so that their futures can be much more secure.

> When has the Holy Spirit nudged you to help another person? Did you witness the positive results of your obedience? Explain.

SAVING A FUTURE KING

We find a story of rescue tucked away in 2 Kings 11. Here's the cast of characters:

- King Ahaziah—king of Judah

- Jehoiada—the priest

- Jehosheba—King Ahaziah's sister and Jehoiada's wife

- Joash—King Ahaziah's son

- Athalia—King Ahaziah's mother

Read 2 Kings 11:1-3.

This rescue story takes place around 841 BC. King Ahaziah ruled in Judah, but for only one year before he was wounded in battle and died (2 Kings 9:27). His mother, Athaliah, wielded a strong influence in the king's court and not in a positive way, bringing worship of the pagan god Baal into court life. When her son died, Athaliah moved swiftly to seize power by having all the male heirs killed.

Jehosheba reacted swiftly to Athaliah's treachery and rescued Joash, the king's infant son, along with the nurse who cared for the baby, and she hid them in the temple. Athaliah ruled in Judah for six years, while Jehosheba and Jehoiada the priest kept Joash safe from harm.

> Oftentimes, being a rescuer means making a sacrifice. What sacrifices did Jehosheba make in rescuing her nephew, the king's son, from the evil Athaliah? What are you willing to sacrifice to be a rescuer?

A FAR-REACHING RESCUE

The first three verses of 2 Kings 11 sound like a simple story of palace intrigue, deception, and treachery. But laid against the canvas of history, the story of Jehosheba and her rescue of Joash is much more than just palace drama. Joash is part of the lineage of King David—a family line that ultimately leads to Jesus, Savior and King. So when Jehosheba acted with bold courage to rescue Joash, she was doing much more than saving a baby boy. She was keeping Jesus' royal lineage intact and helping to fulfill the promise God had made to Jacob several generations earlier:

> "The scepter will not depart from Judah or the staff
> from between his feet until he whose right it is comes
> and the obedience of the peoples belongs to him."
> **GENESIS 49:10**

It was not humanly possible for Jehosheba to have known all that she was accomplishing when she rescued the baby Joash. But God knew, and she was a part of God's plan.

Rescue can take on different forms. You might know someone with physical needs who is waiting for rescue. You might know someone with spiritual needs who is waiting for rescue.

Jot down a name of someone you know who needs some kind of rescue today. Matthew

Maybe the person is struggling with debt, illness, harmful relationships, fear, loss, discouragement, or hopelessness.

What are you able to do to provide rescue for that person today?

WE ALL NEED A RESCUER

Ultimately, all of us need a rescuer, and God provides that rescue for us through Jesus' sacrifice on the cross. Colossians 1:13-14 tells us,

> "He has rescued us from the domain of darkness and
> transferred us into the kingdom of the Son he loves.
> In him we have redemption, the forgiveness of sins."

Because Jesus rescued us, we have the hope that so many are searching for. He is the hero. We need to remember that. The only way we are able to contribute to the rescue of others is because He rescued us. When we're given the opportunity to be a part of rescue—be it physically, emotionally, or spiritually—let's remember to point people to Jesus, the great Rescuer.

IN YOUR OWN WORDS: Reflecting on the story of Jehosheba and her efforts to save baby Joash, how would you define rescue?

IN YOUR OWN LIFE: What steps can you take toward building a legacy of rescue right now?

DAY 4 **RESCUE: RAHAB**

God is in the business of using unlikely people to accomplish His work. Think of Abraham, who was old; Moses, who wasn't a public speaker; David, who committed adultery and murder; Gideon, who was afraid; Matthew, who was a tax collector; or Saul, who was on a mission to persecute Christians. Even in spite of their faults, God used these people to accomplish great things in His kingdom.

Rahab was one of those unlikely people, yet God used her in a mighty way. The King James Version of the Bible describes her as a "harlot." More modern translations like the Christian Standard Bible, the New International Version, and the English Standard Version, all refer to Rahab as a "prostitute."

Read Joshua 2:1-7.

The story of Rahab takes place soon after Moses died. Joshua was leading the people of Israel as they prepared to cross the Jordan River into Canaan. Following God's lead, Joshua and the people would take control of the land through battles and conquest. The first city the people of Israel needed to conquer was Jericho. So Joshua sent two spies to gather information about the city's strength. That's where Rahab enters the story.

The two spies arrived in Jericho and needed a place to hide. Rahab was a prostitute, but she was also an innkeeper, so she gave the men a place to stay.[61]

ROOFTOP PROTECTION
Whispers of the spies' presence in the city reached the ears of the king of Jericho, so the king sent word to Rahab to "bring out the men who came to you and entered your house" (Josh. 2:3). At that moment Rahab

faced a huge decision—produce the men who were hiding inside her house or defy the king's order.

When you face big decisions, whom do you turn to for advice?

How do you decide what to do?

The Bible account gives us no clue as to what Rahab was thinking at the moment she heard the king's order. All we know is that she made a quick decision and lied to protect the two spies. She told a story about the men coming to her house: she didn't know who they were or where they were from, and they left at nightfall before the city gate closed. Then Rahab urged the king's men, "Chase after them quickly, and you can catch up with them!" (v. 5). Rahab evidently did a good job of telling her story because the king's men rushed out of the city gates and headed toward the Jordan River. Meanwhile, back at the inn, the two spies were safely hidden up on the roof under stalks of flax.

How did Rahab show:
Courage?

Selflessness?

Creativity?

Problem-solving skills?

Compassion?

Boldness and bravery?

Quick thinking?

Faith?

Which of these strengths has God given you that you could use to rescue others?

Read Joshua 2:8-11.

With the king's men moving fast away from Rahab's inn, Rahab and the two spies had an interesting conversation.

What do you discover about Rahab's understanding of God in verses 8-11?

What is the bold confession Rahab makes in verse 9?

What is the bold confession Rahab makes in verse 11?

How did Rahab's understanding of God lead her to rescue the spies?

Read Joshua 2:12-14.

Following her bold confessions in verses 9 and 11—"the LORD has given you this land" and "the LORD your God is God in heaven above and on earth below"—Rahab made a bold request of the spies.

Because she had rescued them, what did Rahab ask of the two men in verses 12-13?

Notice that Rahab did not ask that her life be saved, but that the lives of her family be spared. She continued to show her strength as a rescuer.

What did the two spies promise Rahab?

THAT SCARLET CORD
Read Joshua 2:15-21.

Rahab's house was built into the city wall, so to help the spies escape she lowered a rope out the window and the men slid down, leaving the city and running to freedom. Rahab even gave the men suggestions on where to hide and how long to wait before leaving the region.

What were the last instructions the spies gave Rahab before they left (vv. 17-20)?

If you read the rest of the story in Joshua 6, you'll see that Rahab did exactly as the spies instructed. She gathered her family to her house, tied the scarlet cord to her window, and thus provided a way to safety for her whole family when the walls of Jericho fell and the Israelites conquered the city.

Rahab is one of those Old Testament characters who also finds her way into the New Testament. The simple story of Rahab is that she rescued the spies, and in turn, the spies provided a way of rescue for Rahab and her family. But when we read the genealogy of Jesus—the greatest Rescuer of all—in Matthew 1, we find Rahab's name listed in the family line reaching from Abraham to Jesus (v. 5). A prostitute from the pagan city of Jericho became part of the Messiah's family tree. Only God could imagine such a beautiful story of rescue and redemption.

Why would some people have viewed Rahab as an unlikely rescuer?

Most of us quickly agree that God uses unlikely people all the time, but too many of us never include ourselves in that group. Why? What do you think disqualifies you from being used by God?

The truth is that there's nothing in your life that God cannot redeem, forgive, strengthen, and change so that you are equipped for service in His kingdom.

REMEMBERED FOR HER FAITH

Rahab gets another mention in the New Testament where the heroes of the faith are listed:

> "By faith Rahab the prostitute welcomed the spies in peace and didn't perish with those who disobeyed."
> **HEBREWS 11:31**

Rahab, a foreigner and a prostitute, was commended for her faith alongside giants of the faith like Noah, Abraham, Joseph, and Moses.

You may never be called upon to rescue spies on the run from a mad king. But God will bring people across your path who need a helping hand of rescue—from poverty, slavery, addiction, oppression, and especially rescue from sin and death. What do you need to be doing today to be ready to rescue those in need or to point them to the Rescuer?

IN YOUR OWN WORDS: Would you consider yourself an unlikely rescuer? If so, why? How has Jesus equipped you for the work of rescue?

IN YOUR OWN LIFE: What evidence is there in your life that you are building a legacy of rescue? What steps will you take to expand that legacy?

DAY 5 **COMPASSION & RESCUE**

This week we've explored compassion by looking at an Old Testament and New Testament example—Pharaoh's daughter's compassion for baby Moses and Jesus' compassion for a grieving widow. We learned how compassion is more than a feeling. It involves seeing another's need and then acting to relieve that person's suffering.

We've also looked at rescue—physical rescue where lives were saved. Jehosheba rescued the baby and future king Joash, while Rahab rescued the spies which led to the rescue of her family. There are times we can offer rescue to meet physical needs, like food for hungry people, water for thirsty people, money for those in need, or shelter for those far from home. There are other times when rescue involves meeting emotional and spiritual needs—encouraging a discouraged person, calming a frightened person, or sharing the great news of how God rescued you with someone who needs to hear the gospel message.

When we consider legacy ideals like compassion and rescue, we find the best examples in looking to God. He demonstrated both compassion and rescue for us when He sent us a Savior who meets all our needs.

Recall the ways you've seen God move in your life, and record examples below:

I've seen God's compassion expressed in my life through ...

I've seen God's rescue expressed in my life through ...

Reflecting on God's compassion and His rescue at work in our own lives helps us see ways to show compassion and rescue to those we encounter each day.

WEAR COMPASSION

Paul instructs us to "put on compassion" in Colossians 3:12:

> "Therefore, as God's chosen ones, holy and
> dearly loved, put on compassion, kindness,
> humility, gentleness, and patience."

How can you put on compassion each day?

Ask yourself who needs your help and what you can do to help. Where do you see God giving you opportunities to show compassion right now?

REACH OUT TO RESCUE

We all love a rescue story. The firefighter pulls a child from a burning building. Someone in a boat lifts a family from rising floodwaters. The lifeguard drags a struggling swimmer from the riptide. Perhaps we will never see the opportunity to rescue in such a dramatic fashion, but we do have opportunities to be rescuers. There are people in need all around us.

The Bible speaks to the care we are to provide for widows and orphans (Jas. 1:27). In the ancient world, these people would have been the weakest in the community, because the protection a husband and father provided had been stripped away. Think about the people who are vulnerable in your communities today—widows, orphans, those in foster care, those in poverty, the unborn, the elderly, immigrants, those caught in the web of human trafficking. Where will you step in and provide help for them?

People might also need rescue because of overwhelming emotional needs—discouragement, disappointment, hopelessness, or loneliness. How can you step in to lend emotional support or help connect someone to the counseling support they might need?

The very best thing we carry with us is our story of how Jesus, the great Rescuer, has rescued us from sin and adopted us into the family of God. Everyone we meet can benefit from hearing that rescue story.

> In what ways could you lend a hand of rescue to someone in need today?

As you think about building a legacy of compassion and rescue in the days ahead, commit the following verses to memory:

> "It is because of the LORD's lovingkindnesses
> that we are not consumed,
> Because His [tender] compassions never fail.
> They are new every morning;
> Great and beyond measure is Your faithfulness!"
> **LAMENTATIONS 3:22-23, AMP**

session four:

PRAYER &
TENACITY

WATCH

To watch the free video of Session Four, go to LifeWay.com/LegacyStudy.

DISCUSS

What is one thing that stood out to you from the video?

What does it mean to be tenacious?

Would you say that you are tenacious in your praying? Explain.

Besides in our prayer lives, how will being tenacious help us in our spiritual lives?

How much time each day do you spend praying for others? Should it be more? Less? Explain.

Jackie stated, "Some of the best work you will ever do in laying down the foundation for a life of legacy will be done on your knees." What does she mean, and do you agree? Why or why not?

INTRODUCTION

"The joy which answers to prayer give, cannot be described; and the impetus which they afford to the spiritual life is exceedingly great."[62]
GEORGE MUELLER

George Mueller earned his place in history for starting orphanages in England in the 1800s. The orphanage he established in Bristol, England expanded to include five orphanages that cared for two thousand children. It was no small feat at that time. But even more remarkable was the way Mueller managed the funding for his enterprise. You might say it ran on prayer. Mueller never asked for charity. He simply prayed for what the orphanages needed and saw God provide through various people and means. Indeed, Mueller was probably as famous for his effective praying as for his social work. His life exemplified faith-filled, persistent prayer. One example he detailed in his diary, commenting on how he prayed for five specific individuals over time.

It was November 1844 when Mueller felt led to pray for the conversion of these five people he knew. He wrote, "I prayed every day without a single intermission, whether sick or in health, on land or at sea, and whatever the pressure of my engagements might be."[63] It was a year and a half before Mueller saw the first of the five come to Christ. He thanked God for the answer to prayer and continued praying for the others every day. Five years passed before the second person came to faith. Again, Mueller thanked God and kept praying daily for the remaining three people. Six years went by before Mueller saw another answer to prayer among the five.

He kept tenaciously praying for the last two. After almost thirty-six years of praying daily for the salvation of these five people, Mueller wrote, "These two remain unconverted. ... The man to whom God in the riches of his grace has given tens of thousands of answers to prayer in the self-same hour or day in which they were offered has been praying day by day for nearly thirty-six years for the conversion of these individuals, and yet they remain unconverted."[64] According to Mueller's biographer, one of the men Mueller was praying for turned to Christ before Mueller's death and the other a few years after his death.

When have you seen God powerfully answer prayer in your life or someone else's life?

DAY 1 **PRAYER: HANNAH**

THE "GIFT" OF A PROBLEM YOU CANNOT SOLVE

The pain that we cannot bear alone, the circumstances beyond our control, the problems we cannot solve in our own strength—these are gifts. They can drive us to our knees. They can move us to seek our Father, who is our strength and comfort and has all power. These gifts help us recognize what we should have known all along, that we are helpless without Him. And the only way to live is in constant dependence on Him who is our life.

Hannah learned the lesson of dependence on her heavenly Father when she suffered the pain of childlessness. Her sorrow became the gift that drove her to the only One she knew could help her.

> Read 1 Samuel 1:1-16. What was Hannah's problem she could not solve?

> How did the people around her contribute to her difficult situation?

Childlessness has always been a difficult issue for any woman who wants to be a mother and can't conceive. But in ancient times, there was also a stigma attached to infertility. A woman's value was tied to her ability to produce heirs for her husband. Most women didn't devote their lives to education, career, *and* family. There was only family. If they failed to produce children, they had failed in their purpose. And without children to support them in their old age, they could experience the sting of poverty as well.

WHAT ONLY GOD KNOWS

Reread verses 5-6. Why was Hannah unable to conceive according to these verses?

The Bible teaches that in some situations God allows His people to encounter certain difficulties so we will turn to Him. Then, He can demonstrate His power and faithfulness. How He does that differs from one situation to another.

In John 9:1-6, Jesus and His disciples came upon a man who had been blind from birth. Jesus' disciples asked Him why the man had been born blind, whether it was because the man sinned or his parents before him. "Neither this man nor his parents sinned," Jesus said. "This came about so that God's works might be displayed in him" (v. 3). Then Jesus spread mud over the man's eyes, restoring his sight and astonishing his neighbors.

In 1 Samuel 1:9-11 we see Hannah turning to God with her problem. How would you characterize her prayer?

This probably wasn't the first time Hannah had gone to God with her problem. She may have prayed about it for a long time. But there was some point in time when she recognized she was confronting a situation that wasn't going to get better on its own. She couldn't get the help she needed from her husband. And she couldn't fix it herself. The only One who could help her was God, so she turned to Him.

When have you found yourself in that place?

GOD HEARS THE HUMBLE

Broken and humbled by her powerlessness, Hannah was in the perfect place to approach God and beg for His mercy. God hates pride and punishes arrogance (Prov. 8:13; 2 Kings 19:28). But He listens to those who come humbly to Him for help.

> "LORD, you have heard the desire of the humble;
> You will strengthen their hearts.
> You will listen carefully."
> **PSALM 10:17**

Hannah's request held no sense of entitlement. There was no "You owe me this" or "I deserve this" or "It's my right." In fact, she even offered to give the child back to God if He would make her a mother.

What were the specific details of her vow (v. 11)?

It seems part of Hannah's vow included dedicating her son to the Lord as a lifelong Nazarite (Num. 6:1-21). Her promise never to cut his hair parallels the commitment Samson made as a Nazarite (Judg. 13:5-7).

NOBODY KNOWS THE TROUBLE I'VE SEEN

Read 1 Samuel 1:12-18. How helpful would you say Eli the priest was to Hannah throughout their encounter?

Eli, the high priest at Shiloh, misunderstood Hannah's pleading at first and rebuked her, thinking she was intoxicated. He was a spiritual leader, but he misread Hannah's pain. His response reminds us that sometimes nobody will get your problems but God. Only the One who made you fully understands what you're going through and what you need.

In verses 17-18, Hannah's circumstances had not yet changed, but she had. What made the difference?

How do you think the following Scripture verses apply to Hannah's situation?
1 Peter 5:7

Psalm 34:18

John 16:24b

Matthew 7:7-11

John 14:27

Write out one of the previous Scripture passages that is the most meaningful to you in your current circumstances.

Verses 19-28 of 1 Samuel 1 tell how God answered Hannah's prayer "after some time" (v. 20). What is significant about that phrase?

As stated earlier, this urgent pleading from Hannah recorded in 1 Samuel 1 probably wasn't the only time Hannah had prayed for a child. But it was in that moment, at that time, that the Lord chose to answer by granting her request. God works in His time, in His way, according to His will. He always answers our prayers—not always the way we want or when we want. But He does answer.

Hannah named her baby Samuel. In Hebrew, reversing the first two letters of his name creates a word that means "He who was asked for."[65] Acrostically, Samuel can be derived from a Hebrew name that means "asked from God."[66] Once Samuel was weaned, Hannah kept her vow, bringing her son to Eli to serve God in the temple. He would become Israel's greatest (and last) judge at a critical period in their history.[67]

> What is the deepest concern in your heart today? Have you brought that request before God? If so, how have you seen Him answer your request (even if He hasn't answered the way you want)?

PRAYER IS SEEKING GOD, NOT SEEKING STUFF
Read 1 Samuel 2:1-11.

Prayer is not like sending Santa Claus our wish list, just so we can get what we want. It's not even like visiting the psychiatrist and telling him all our problems, so he can tell us how to fix them. God does care about the details of our lives. He gives good gifts and helps us with our problems. But more than that, prayer is where we encounter the living God and come to understand who He is. We don't shape Him to see our will; He shapes us to see His.

When Hannah returned to the place where she had previously poured out her heart in sorrow to God, her prayer revealed what she had come to know about God.

> List several things about God—who He is and what He does—that Hannah expressed she had learned from her experience.

What have you learned about who God is through answered prayer?

Hannah's life was a testimony to the truths she proclaimed, that God delivers those who trust Him. Her example of earnest prayer became her legacy. She is the only woman in the Old Testament specifically mentioned for her praying. She is the only woman who made a vow to God.[68] God used her petition to provide the nation of Israel one of its greatest leaders. And in the process, He demonstrated His power to hear and help those who come to Him in faith.

IN YOUR OWN WORDS: Based on what you've studied today, how would you define prayer?

IN YOUR OWN LIFE: What is the next step God is challenging you to take toward building a legacy of prayer?

DAY 2 **PRAYER**

*"God will either give us what we ask
or give us what we would have asked
if we knew everything he knows."*[69]
TIMOTHY KELLER

WHEN JESUS DIDN'T SHOW UP

When it comes to prayer, we love to quote verses like John 16:23-24, which says, "Truly I tell you, anything you ask the Father in my name, he will give you. ... Ask and you will receive, so that your joy may be complete." If this were the only thing the Bible said about prayer, we might believe prayer is supposed to be a blank check for us to get whatever we want, whenever we want. When we don't get what we want immediately, we might think we just need to be persistent in asking, as we learned in yesterday's lesson.

But anyone who has walked with God very long or read the Bible knows that's not how prayer works. What Jesus said in John 16:23-24 is true, but it is only part of the truth. Prayer is deeper and more complex than just asking and automatically receiving what you want every time.

This principle is plain to see in the way Jesus interacted with two of his closest friends, Mary and Martha, the sisters of Lazarus. The three of them knew Jesus well. So when Lazarus got really sick, the two sisters took for granted that just sending word of their brother's illness would bring Jesus running immediately. Their brief message simply stated, "Lord, the one you love is sick" (John 11:3). That's all. There was no asking or begging. The response was assumed. It was like praying, "I have no food or money" or "My child is missing." Presenting the urgent need alone assumes the caring, all-powerful Lord will meet the need appropriately. And for Mary and Martha, "appropriately" would have meant coming quickly and healing Lazarus the way Jesus had healed so many other people. But He didn't come immediately. And Lazarus died.

> Read John 11:1-44. How do these events from the lives of Mary and Martha relate to the Timothy Keller quote at the beginning of this session?

> When have you been in a similar place in your prayer life?

THE BLESSING OF UNANSWERED PRAYER

Developing a legacy of prayer truly means learning to pray with faith and persistence. It is about coming to God with bold faith like Hannah and humbly seeking His help. But becoming a legacy pray-er is also growing in our faith to the point that we understand praying is bowing to God's will and not bending Him to ours. For the teachable, prayer can be the life school where we learn that God's ways are higher than our ways and His thoughts are higher than our thoughts (Isa. 55:9).

> What's one prayer you've prayed that you're glad God didn't answer the way you wanted Him to?

> Read 2 Corinthians 12:6-10.

Much speculation has been made regarding what Paul's "thorn in the flesh" (v. 7) actually was. Theories include:

- physical ailments (like poor eyesight or a chronic illness);

- psychological or spiritual issues (like depression, some sort of demonic oppression, or chronic temptation from a physical desire);

- opposition to his ministry (both inside and outside the churches).[70]

In the end, no one really knows. That may be a good thing, because it makes it easier to substitute your own problem that won't go away and doesn't get any better no matter how long you've prayed about it.

Notice Paul prayed repeatedly and asked God to remove this problem from his life. Whatever the issue, you can imagine Paul's rationale. Any such problem could distract him from his ministry. It wasn't just about his comfort or convenience; he had an important role in the gospel mission. This thing was holding him back. It was preventing him from operating at his full potential. Or was it?

Write God's response to Paul (v. 9a) in the space provided below:

How would you explain God's response?

What ironic truth did Paul come to discover through God's answer (vv. 9b-10)?

ASKING BUT ACCEPTING
Read Matthew 26:36-46.

It can be frustrating to pray for something and not get the answer you want. Even Jesus asked the Father for something—"My Father, if it is possible, let this cup pass from me" (Matt. 26:39)—and didn't get the answer He wanted. Jesus knew of the torture and death that awaited Him long before He was arrested and tried (Matt. 17:22-23; 20:17-19; Luke 9:22; 18:31-33), and He prayed for another way to accomplish God's plan. He knew full well He would bear the sins of the world on the cross and in so doing alienate Himself in that moment from His holy Father (1 Pet. 2:24; Mark 15:33-34).

How did Jesus describe His feelings about His situation (vv. 37-38)?

What was Jesus' request in prayer? How many times did He ask?

"Cup" in the Old Testament is a symbol for God's wrath and judgment (Ps. 75:7-8; Isa. 51:17). The cup Jesus wanted to pass on was the fury of God's punishment against sin. He was asking if there was any other way to provide forgiveness other than the crucifixion He saw before Him.

How did Jesus model the truth that prayer is about discovering God's will and not getting God to do ours?

Read Matthew 26:47-54.

Notice what Jesus told His disciples who tried to defend Him when the Roman guards came to arrest Him. Jesus was not only fully human; He was fully God. He had all of heaven at His command. He did not have to submit to God's plan, yet He did. And He modeled for us what it means to truly communicate with God in prayer.

What do you learn about prayer based on Jesus' example in both of these passages? Does this change or reinforce what you previously believed about prayer?

Why do you think God didn't grant His Son's request?

How might things be different if He had?

In our time, Joni Eareckson Tada serves as one of the most powerful examples of God's power at work through the life of a woman who accepted God's will over her prayer request. In July 1967, then seventeen-year-old Joni suffered a diving accident that left her a quadriplegic. Joni prayed for healing. She explained, "When I was first injured, I just wanted out of my wheelchair. I wanted to walk again, I wanted to have hands that worked. So I followed every Scriptural injunction: I was anointed with oil, I went to the elders, I confessed sin."[71] She went to healing services. But the praying and believing and all the rest didn't change anything. More than fifty years later, Joni remains paralyzed. Additionally, she endured breast cancer and severe chronic pain. And yet, Joni said she came to see there were more important things in life than being able to walk or use your hands, things like having a heart free of the grip of sin and pride and self-centeredness.

Through Joni's unanswered prayer, God did a work in her life that transformed her from the inside out. And she has become a world changer for the kingdom of God. She leads an international ministry, advocates for people with disabilities, is a popular speaker, best-selling author, and radio host.[72] Author Philip Yancey writes of Joni, "Through her public example, Joni has done more to straighten out warped views of suffering than all the theologians put together. Her life is a triumph of healing—a healing of the spirit, the most difficult kind."[73]

It's easy to see in our two days of study that prayer is not simply giving God a list of requests and Him fulfilling those. Rather, prayer is a divine, intimate conversation whereby we talk to God and He speaks to us. We know Him better through prayer. Our lives are changed through prayer. We gain a clearer understanding of His purpose through prayer. He may not always answer how or when we want, but we can know that God faithfully and powerfully works through prayer. Be diligent to leave a legacy of prayer.

IN YOUR OWN WORDS: Based on what you've studied today, how would you define prayer?

IN YOUR OWN LIFE: What is the next step God is challenging you to take toward building a legacy of prayer?

DAY 3 **TENACITY:**

THE SYROPHOENICIAN WOMAN

> *"Our greatest weakness lies in giving up. The most certain way to succeed is always try just one more time."*[74]
> THOMAS EDISON

Thomas Edison was famous for his perseverance. When he was trying to invent the incandescent light bulb, he made more than a thousand attempts before he succeeded. A local newspaper reporter questioned him about his many failures. Without missing a beat, Edison replied, "I didn't fail. I simply found a thousand ways not to make a light bulb."[75] Ultimately, Edison became one of America's most famous inventors, credited with creating not only the incandescent light bulb but also the telegraph, the phonograph, the universal stock ticker, alkaline storage batteries, and the Kinetograph (a camera for motion pictures). He came to hold more than a thousand patents for his inventions. History views him as having helped build the U.S. economy during its early years. There is no doubt he left a legacy. Clearly his tenacity is the reason why.

Call it tenacity, perseverance, grit, or determination. It's that quality in us that refuses to give up even when things look bad. It's what motivates us to keep hoping against hopelessness. It's the passion that drives us to keep moving toward our goals no matter what because we've already decided we will not be deterred.

Just as tenacious people impact history in other areas of life, tenacious Christ followers leave a spiritual legacy with their never-give-up attitude.

What's something you quit that you now wish you had stayed with longer?

REFUSING TO GIVE UP

Read Matthew 15:21-28.

Jesus withdrew to the region of Tyre and Sidon, which was Gentile territory, in order to escape the pressure of the Pharisees. Jesus didn't avoid Gentiles the way most Jews did, but His ministry up to this point was primarily focused on "the lost sheep of the house of Israel" (v. 24). On this day, however, His ministry was interrupted by an extremely determined Gentile woman on a mission of her own.

> What was the woman's goal? What did she do initially to get Jesus' help in accomplishing that goal?

The Christian Standard Bible translation says she "kept crying out, 'Have mercy on me, Lord, Son of David!'" (v. 22). In other words, she wouldn't be quiet! Over and over, she continued crying out to Jesus to help her.

> Reread verse 23. How did Jesus respond to this woman? How did the disciples respond?

The very fact that the woman addressed Jesus as "Lord, Son of David" shows she recognized Him as the Messiah. It's possible she was a Greek convert. It was not unheard of for some Gentiles to convert to Judaism. But what's clear is that she had a very big problem and she fully believed Jesus was capable of making it right. With the one and only Person who could heal her daughter right there in her presence, the woman refused to give up until Jesus responded to her plea.

How did Jesus appear to test the woman's persistence?

At first glance, this passage makes Jesus seem harsh and uncaring. In verse 24, He told the Gentile woman He had come only to the lost sheep of Israel. This has to be taken in context. Jesus ministered to Gentiles many other times (Matt. 4:24-25; 8:5-13), and He clearly taught that His death was for all people (Matt. 28:19-20). He was saying here that He came first to the Jews, who would have the opportunity to bring the gospel to the rest of the world. Then in verse 26, Jesus used a parable about not feeding the children's bread to the dogs. He wasn't degrading the woman, comparing her to a dog. Rather, the parable illustrated the order of things. The children ate before the pets. Similarly, Jesus had His priorities.

How did the woman meet Jesus' test each time He provided her a reason to give up?

How did Jesus ultimately respond to the woman's refusal to take no for an answer? Why was Jesus so pleased with this woman's response?

Here's the hard part—how is this woman's situation different from the prayers we learned about in the last session, where mature believers (Paul, Jesus) learned to accept God's no?

When does great faith keep asking and when does it accept that God has a better way than what we want?

This is a difficult question to answer. Perhaps we keep seeking, asking, and knocking (Matt. 7:7-8) until we get a definitive answer. Paul kept asking until he received a definitive no. The woman in this story persisted until she received a definitive yes. But know this: regardless of how long we wait for an answer or what that answer ends up being, God is working all things for His glory and our good (Rom. 8:28). In the praying and the waiting He is accomplishing His purpose in us—making us more like Jesus.

WHEN YOU DON'T SEE CHANGE COMING

Read Luke 18:1-8. When have you waited a long time for change to come? How long did you wait?

It's significant that the parable of the persistent widow immediately follows Jesus' discussion of His coming kingdom (17:20-27). When Christ's kingdom comes, He will be exalted and evil will be conquered. But between now and then, in this in-between time, there is suffering and injustice. We are waiting for the world's wrongs to be righted. And we pray as Jesus taught us to pray, "Your kingdom come. Your will be done on earth as it is in heaven" (Matt. 6:10).

When Jesus told the parable of the persistent widow, He was speaking to first-century Jews under the yoke of Roman oppression, who were waiting for their Messiah to set them free. And throughout the ages He's been speaking to the poor, who are waiting for the day they won't have to worry about feeding their families. He's speaking to the sick and suffering and those under oppression of all types. He's speaking to every person who holds to the hope of His return. Jesus speaks to all of us who look to God for whatever change we long for. And His message is this: "Don't give up."

What is the point of the parable (v. 1)?

How did the widow in the story demonstrate tenacity?

How is the judge in the story unlike God? What did he do that is like God?

In the last session, we learned that prayer is about shaping our wills to God's will.

Was Jesus saying in this parable that if we just keep bugging God long enough, eventually He'll give us what we want even if it's not what He wants? If not, what is He saying?

At its root, this parable speaks to holding fast to faith in God. It speaks to refusing to give up seeking His help even when we don't see change coming. Jesus said it like this in Matthew 7:7-8 (NLT):

"Keep on asking, and you will receive what you ask for. Keep on seeking, and you will find. Keep on knocking, and the door will be opened to you. For everyone who asks, receives. Everyone who seeks, finds. And to everyone who knocks, the door will be opened."

What assumption did Jesus make about human nature when He told us to "keep on" asking, seeking, and knocking?

WHERE ELSE WOULD WE GO?

Skim John 6:60-68. Why did many of Jesus' followers begin to leave at this point? Why did Simon Peter and the other eleven disciples stay?

Tenacious faith is grounded in the truth that Jesus Christ is our only hope. We never give up seeking Him because we recognize He alone is the all-loving, all-powerful God who will never let us down.

How would you explain to someone who doesn't know God why you will never quit believing in Him for the help you need?

IN YOUR OWN WORDS: Based on what you've studied today, how would you define tenacity?

IN YOUR OWN LIFE: Would you say that you currently have tenacious faith? Why or why not?

DAY 4 **TENACITY**

"Whatever you do, find the God-centered, Christ-exalting, Bible-saturated passion of your life, and find your way to say it and live for it and die for it. And you will make a difference that lasts. You will not waste your life."[76]
JOHN PIPER

Agnes Gonxha Bojaxhiu is not famous because she had a reality TV show. She wasn't a movie star or a supermodel. She's not known for writing best-selling books or recording chart-topping songs. But then, she never aspired to win a popularity contest with the world. Instead, as an 18-year-old, she left home to join an Irish community of nuns with missions in India. On May 24, 1931, she took her vows to become a nun. After teaching high school in Calcutta from 1931 to 1948, she left her teaching position to work helping the poorest of the poor in the slums of Calcutta. Others joined her in her passion. And in 1950, she founded "The Missionaries of Charity" with the purpose of caring for persons no one else would help—refugees, the homeless, those with AIDS, alcoholics, and shut-ins. By 1997, when she died, Agnes, whom the world knows as Mother Teresa, had been recognized with many prestigious accolades, including the Nobel Peace Prize for her life's work among the poor of Calcutta.[77]

Toward the end of Mother Teresa's life, journalist Renzo Allegri, who had interviewed her many times, was chatting with her again and asked spontaneously, "Are you afraid of dying?"[78] When Mother Teresa seemed puzzled at the reason for his question, Allegri tried to explain, "In recent years you have undergone some rather delicate surgical interventions, such as the one on the heart; you must take care of yourself, travel less." To this she responded, "Everyone says this to me, but I must think of the work that Jesus has entrusted to me. When I can no longer serve, he will stop me."[79]

And then, reflecting again on what it would mean to die, the aged Christ follower mused, "I would be as happy as you if I could say that I will die this evening. Dying I too would go home. I would go to paradise. I would go to meet Jesus. I have consecrated my life to Jesus. ... All that I do here, on this earth, I do it out of love for him. ... How can I be afraid of death? I desire it; I await it because it allows me finally to return home."[80]

> What does the phrase "finish well" mean to you? How do you apply that to your spiritual life?

ON RUNNING WELL

> Read Hebrews 12:1. The author of Hebrews spoke of the Christian life as a race. Did he consider this life a sprint or a marathon? How do you know? Would you agree? Why or why not?

Maybe you've watched or even run a marathon, like the Boston Marathon or the Marine Corps Marathon. You've seen the crowds lining the roads, especially toward the finish line, cheering the runners on. In the Christian life we also have cheerleaders, a cloud of witnesses. These faithful believers who have gone on before us are not watching down from above as mere spectators. The testimony of their faithfulness cheers us on; their example encourages us to keep running to the end.[81]

Marathon runners carry no extra weight. Their clothing is as light-weight as possible. On cold race days, runners commonly dress in layers and drop outer clothing along the route during the race as they get warmer. They carry no extraneous gear that could hinder their progress.

Everything is planned with the intention of making it across that finish line. Likewise, the writer of Hebrews said that in the Christian life we mustn't carry things that slow us down or cause us to falter. Sin is an obvious impediment to achieving God's purpose for our lives. But even good things can distract us from our primary purpose.

How could the following things distract you from making God and His purpose the priority of your life?

Relationships

Entertainment

Achievement

Work/Career

Use of Time

Money/Possessions

Social Media

Which of these is currently weighing you down? How?

THE BEST LIFE EVER LIVED

Read Hebrews 12:2.

Jesus is the one Person who always chose right. He always obeyed God. He always had His priorities in order. He is the only Person who could look back on His life and say, "There's nothing I should have done differently." He demonstrated for us an unwavering determination to glorify God by living every day of His life for the purpose God had for Him.

CONSIDER HIS LIFE

What are most twelve-year-old boys interested in? At twelve, what was Jesus interested in (Luke 2:41-50)?

How did Jesus respond when tempted to compromise His purpose (Matt. 4:1-11)?

Read Matthew 16:21-23.

Jesus was explaining to His disciples God's plan for His life, that He had come to die. Peter, who always seemed to speak for the group, took Jesus aside and tried to talk Him out of it.

How did Jesus respond in verse 23 that showed He was tenacious about not being distracted from God's purpose for Him?

Read Luke 9:51-55. Write the phrase that describes how Jesus set out for Jerusalem as He saw His time approaching.

Jesus knew what awaited Him in Jerusalem (Luke 9:21-22; 43-44), yet He never wavered from the mission and purpose of His life on earth.

Why do you think He was so determined to keep moving toward the danger of those who were plotting to kill Him?

Jesus could have quit His mission …

- When the Pharisees started to oppose Him (Mark 2:16);

- When His own family members misunderstood Him and thought He was out of His mind (Mark 3:20-21);

- When He was arrested, and His disciples fled (Matt. 26:56);

- When He stood before His accusers on trumped-up charges but remained silent (Matt. 26:57-63);

- Anywhere between the garden of Gethsemane and the cross when He could have called legions of angels to set Him free (Matt. 26:52-53).

But He never quit.

GOD STICKS WITH US
Reread Hebrews 12:2.

You and I will not run a perfect race. We will not look back on our lives and be able to say like Jesus, "There's nothing I should have done differently." But we can finish well what God has laid out for us to do. We can finish strong not because *we* are strong but because *Jesus* is.

Eugene Peterson put it like this, "We survive in the way of faith not because we have extraordinary stamina but because God is righteous, because God sticks with us."[82] Keeping our eyes on the One who is strong and faithful and never wavering allows us to keep keeping on to the end. Our tenacious faith is inspired by Him, found in Him, and empowered by Him.

Read Eugene Peterson's paraphrase of Hebrews 12:1-3 from The Message. Highlight one thing in the passage you will do in order to finish well.

"... Strip down, start running—and never quit! No extra spiritual fat, no parasitic sins. Keep your eyes on Jesus, who both began and finished this race we're in. Study how he did it. Because he never lost sight of where he was headed—that exhilarating finish in and with God— he could put up with anything along the way: Cross, shame, whatever. And now he's there, in the place of honor, right alongside God. When you find yourselves flagging in your faith, go over that story again, item by item, that long litany of hostility he plowed through. That will shoot adrenaline into your souls!"

IN YOUR OWN WORDS: Based on what you've studied today, how would you define finishing well in life?

IN YOUR OWN LIFE: Based on what you've learned today, what is the next step God is challenging you to take toward building a legacy of tenacious faith?

DAY 5 PRAYER & TENACITY

"The Scripture says, 'Pray without ceasing' (1 Thessalonians 5:17). This should be the motto of every true follower of Jesus Christ. Never stop praying, no matter how dark and hopeless your case may seem. Your responsibility isn't to tell God when He must act or even how He must act. Your responsibility is simply to 'pray without ceasing' trusting Him to act according to His perfect will."[83]

BILLY GRAHAM

WHERE TENACITY MEETS PRAYERFULNESS

Prayer is not about getting more *from* God; it is about getting more *of* God. It is where we pursue Him and His will and seek to know His heart. No doubt, prayer is about asking. Jesus told us to ask and we would receive. We looked at the example of Hannah, who prayed for a child and received Samuel. We studied Jesus' parable of the persistent widow, whose example reminds us to keep praying for what we need from God. This is where tenacity meets prayerfulness. But we also saw from the examples of Paul and Jesus that prayer is about submitting to God's better plan when He says no to ours.

When God says no, the mature Christ follower relinquishes the request but continues to pursue God. This is also tenacity. Tenacity in prayer and the pursuit of God means not giving up on Him because He has never given up on us. It means holding fast even when there is no evidence of His presence or help. This is not blind faith; it is well founded on a long history of His kept promises.

The tenacious cry out with Job, "Though he slay me, yet will I hope in Him" (Job 13:15, NIV). They affirm with Paul, "I am suffering. ... Yet this is no cause for shame, because I know whom I have believed, and am convinced that he is able to guard what I have entrusted to him until that day" (2 Tim. 1:12, NIV). This unwavering, enduring, prayerful trust mirrors God's everlasting love for us. It is not normal, and the world takes notice when it appears.

PRAYING BECAUSE HE IS WORTHY

In C. S. Lewis's satire, *The Screwtape Letters*, a senior devil named Uncle Screwtape writes to his younger nephew devil, Wormwood, advising him on how to tempt away from God a man referred to simply as "the patient." Working for Satan and considering God the enemy, Uncle Screwtape advises Wormwood as follows:

> "Our cause is never more in danger than when a
> human, no longer desiring, but still intending to do
> our Enemy's will, looks round upon a universe from
> which every trace of Him seems to have vanished, and
> asks why he has been forsaken, and still obeys."[84]

Lewis's humor and irony make a striking point. When God removes the props that make it easy for us to keep seeking Him, praying to Him, and believing in Him, but we do it anyway, we send a powerful message to the world: "I do not pray to a God who gives me every gift I name and claim. I pray to a God who is the Almighty Creator, who alone is worthy of all worship. He deserves my obedience regardless of my circumstances. I will keep on seeking Him, trusting Him, and praying to Him."

TENACIOUS LEGACY MAKERS

Who were these tenacious people? What was their legacy?
2 Kings 18:1-8:

2 Timothy 4:6-8;16-18:

What tempts you …
To give up or slack off on praying?

To stop believing or serving?

To pursue God less?

What keeps you praying and pursuing God?

How is your tenacity impacting someone else to stick with God to the end?

Commit these verses to memory as you work to build a legacy of prayer and tenacity.

> "Therefore, since we also have such a large cloud of witnesses surrounding us, let us lay aside every hindrance and the sin that so easily ensnares us. Let us run with endurance the race that lies before us, keeping our eyes on Jesus, the source and perfecter of our faith. For the joy that lay before him, he endured the cross, despising the shame, and sat down at the right hand of the throne of God."
> **HEBREWS 12:1-2**

session five:

GENEROSITY
& LOYALTY

WATCH

To watch the free video of Session Five, go to LifeWay.com/LegacyStudy.

DISCUSS

What is one thing that stood out to you from the video?

Who's the most generous person you know?

How are you currently using your resources to further God's kingdom?

Why do you think loyalty is important in leaving behind a godly legacy?

ties into faith .

How do you express your loyalty to Jesus?

Prayer + Faith Share .

How do loyalty and generosity call for sacrifice?

INTRODUCTION

In 1965, Carol Donald took in her first foster child. She and her family lived in northern California. Her own children were in high school and her husband had recently retired from the Air Force. While attending a church class with her daughter, Carol noticed two pregnant girls who were only fourteen and wondered what would happen to the babies when they were born. She prayed about her concerns, and the next day she answered a newspaper ad for foster parent training.

In the years that followed, Carol and her husband were foster parents to one hundred children with medical needs. Some of the babies were born addicted to methadone or suffered from fetal alcohol syndrome, and the Donalds lovingly cared for these babies through terrible seizures.

When her husband died in 1985, Carol didn't stop. Determined to go on caring for foster children, she continued foster parenting for another twenty-three years. Carol finally "retired" as a foster parent when she fell and broke her femur at age eighty-five. "I've put my heart and soul into those children," Carol said.[85] Her foster children call her "Grandma" and they call each other "cousins." Once a year, they gather for a reunion. Carol says, "It's a wonderful life I live, and if I had to live my life over I wouldn't do it one bit differently."[86]

Freely opening her heart, her home, and her life, Carol Donald demonstrated generosity in reaching out to provide and care for some of the most vulnerable children in her community. She modeled generosity in her actions by making a safe home for these children in the foster care system. Truly she has built a legacy of generosity.

Sometimes what comes to mind when we think of leaving a legacy of generosity are those great philanthropists who acquired a lot of wealth and give lots of money to numerous causes. However, we'll see through our study this week that a legacy of generosity is not measured by the amount given but by the attitude of the heart.

When you think of a generous person, who comes to mind? Why that person?

DAY 1 **GENEROSITY: THE POOR WIDOW**

UNPROTECTED AND VULNERABLE

In Mark 12:41-44, we find the story of Jesus sitting and watching the people as they brought their offerings to the temple treasury. The Court of the Women area of the temple—the space that was as close as the women could get to the sanctuary—was where the treasury was located. Consisting of trumpet-shaped chests where worshipers placed their offerings, the sound of the dropping coins was amplified. A large offering amount could make a lot of noise when the worshiper dropped it into the chest.[87]

The Bible also tells us that plenty of wealthy people put in big offerings. At first glance, it might make sense for Jesus to call attention to one of those big, loud offerings if He wanted to talk about generosity. But Jesus often did the unexpected. This time, He called attention to a woman who dropped in just two coins.

As we've mentioned previously in this study, in the ancient world widows were among the weakest, most vulnerable members of society. Men in that culture provided the economic, legal, and physical protection for women and children. A woman whose husband died stood unprotected.

Yet when Jesus wanted to describe generosity and show what it looked like, He looked to the example of a widow.

> Read Mark 12:41-44. What do you think Jesus is teaching us in this story about the widow's offering?

Think about the way God views generosity and
compare it to the way many people in our culture today
view it. How is it similar? How is it different?

SHE GAVE "ALL"

Most of us are fortunate that we have never needed to worry about
having enough money to buy food. But the widow Jesus observed lived
much closer to the edge of going hungry. The phrase "all she had to live
on" (v. 44) meant that she would not have enough for her next meal.

What kinds of honest excuses might the widow have
had for not giving an offering at the temple that day?

Which of the following reasons have you used for not
giving?
☐ "I'll give when I have more."
☐ "I'll give when I get a raise."
☐ "I'll give when I'm older."
☐ "I'll give when my bills are paid down."
☐ Other reasons:

The Bible does not tell us that the woman spoke during this brief time
when Jesus watched her. Yet her actions shout to us from the pages of
Scripture. Through her example, Jesus teaches us that generosity is not
tied to the amount of our financial resources.

Why is your net worth irrelevant when it comes to
being a generous person?

It's important to remember that we can give in a variety of ways. Giving doesn't necessarily mean digging deep into your wallet or checkbook. Consider your many different kinds of resources—all of these are gifts from God. Yes, giving our money is one way we should give. But we can also be generous with our time, energy, talents, resources, and words.

THE FAITH CONNECTION

What was the woman demonstrating when she gave everything she had?

Maybe it feels like it's easy to be generous if we have a lot. In our heads, we connect our ability to give with the balance in our bank accounts. But the Bible teaches that generosity isn't connected to our bank balances—it's connected to our faith.

How is generosity connected to faith in God?

What kind of faith did the woman demonstrate when she gave "all she had to live on"?

How did Jesus redefine greatness with this story of the widow's giving?

In our culture, people are often impressed with "big." Big money gifts are more impressive than tiny money gifts. When Jesus saw the widow give all she had, though, He turned the idea of big upside down and showed us that in God's economy all gifts, large or small, are important.

CHURCHES THAT OVERFLOWED GENEROSITY

We find another beautiful example of generosity in 2 Corinthians 8. This story showcases the bold generosity displayed by churches in the region of Macedonia.

Read 2 Corinthians 8:1-9.

These churches were not wealthy. In fact, they were just the opposite—churches where the members lived in poverty. Paul described how these churches were experiencing "a severe trial brought about by affliction" and "extreme poverty" (v. 2). So perhaps it was an unexpected turn when Paul wrote to the more affluent church in Corinth and named the Macedonian churches as a role model of generosity.

Despite their own poverty, when the believers in the Macedonian churches heard that there was a famine and the believers in Jerusalem were suffering, they dug deep and gave generously (8:10).

Paul said the Macedonian believers gave "beyond their ability" (v. 3) and "begged us earnestly for the privilege of sharing" (v. 4).

Think about times when you had an opportunity to give—did it feel more like a burden, obligation, or privilege? Explain.

How does it impact our attitude and our generosity when we view giving to God's work as a privilege?

THE SECRET SAUCE RECIPE FOR GENEROUS GIVING

How is it that these impoverished Macedonians "overflowed in a wealth of generosity" (v. 2)? How could they be willing to give over and above? The answer seems to lie in a priority action and a prime example.

Reread verse 5. What was the priority action? How does that action affect our generosity?

Reread verse 9. Who was the prime example? How does that example affect our generosity?

When our lives are dedicated to Christ and we understand the depth of His generosity toward us in His sacrificial death, how can we not be generous in return? He showed us the way and we follow with joyful, obedient, legacy-leaving generosity.

IN YOUR OWN WORDS: Reflecting on the passages we studied today, how would you define generosity?

IN YOUR OWN LIFE: What next steps do you need to take toward building a legacy of generosity?

DAY 2 GENEROSITY:

THE SHUNAMMITE WOMAN

In contrast to the widow who gave "all she had to live on"—just two coins—in today's study we see the example of a wealthy woman who also modeled generosity. But the two women, one poor and the other rich, are similar in that the Bible does not tell us their names. Across the centuries we know them only by their stories.

Read 2 Kings 4:8-10.

Not knowing her name, we call her the "Shunammite woman," reflecting the village, Shunem, where she lived. Besides naming the place she lived, the Bible also tells us that she was wealthy. Notice the words used to describe her (v. 8) in different Bible translations: "prominent" (CSB), "well-to-do" (NIV), "prominent and influential" (AMP), "notable" (NKJV), "wealthy" (ESV).

If we feel our resources are limited and money is tight, we might miss opportunities for generosity because of fear we don't have enough. If our resources are plenty and money is not a concern, then what excuses might we give for missing opportunities for generosity?

HABITS OF GENEROSITY
The Shunammite woman must have viewed her wealth as something she could share with others. In the story told in 2 Kings 4, the woman saw God's prophet Elisha passing by her house, so she invited him to stop and eat.

There was nothing spectacular about what she did. It was just a simple act, but it met a need. The seeds of generosity are planted in our hearts when we see the needs around us and then think of ways we can step in to help meet those needs. Verse 8 tells us that the Shunammite woman was soon feeding Elisha "whenever he passed by."

How can you cultivate your initial actions of generosity into habits of generosity, like the Shunammite woman did in feeding Elisha?

In what ways do your habits of generosity build a legacy of generosity in your life?

The Shunammite woman's habit of feeding Elisha whenever he passed by led to an even greater opportunity for generosity.

Review verses 9-10. What was the Shunammite woman's generous next step?

This story is an example of generous giving that didn't involve just giving money. Sure, this woman was wealthy, but she also had food and created a room to share. Plus, she gave her time—time to cook, build the room, furnish it, and clean it in between the times Elisha would have stayed there.

In what other ways could you be generous besides giving your money?

The Shunammite woman saw Elisha and considered his needs—he was hungry and he needed a safe place to sleep. She thought of his comfort.

Read Philippians 2:3-4.

Sometimes our natural inclination is to look out for our own interests first. But we reflect a more Christ-like character when we look out first for the interests of others.

In practical ways, how can you look out for the interests of others?

How does generosity get easier when you put the needs of others ahead of your own?

GENEROUS AQUEDUCTS

In Old Testament times, aqueducts were built to bring water from places where it was plentiful to other places where the water supply was limited. These aqueducts could be very simple in construction—just troughs or ditches dug out of the rock and soil. The city of Jerusalem received its water through a system of aqueducts that brought the spring water from the mountains into the city.

A generous person living a generous life works a lot like an aqueduct—simply being a channel where the blessings God provides are shared with those who have needs. God gives us wealth so we can share it. We are to be channels of His generosity.

How does seeing yourself as an aqueduct of God's blessings challenge your generosity?

SOURCE OF ALL OUR GOOD STUFF

"Sometimes I struggle with generosity because it's hard to let go of my _____."

Just fill in the blank with whatever it is you hold too tightly—your money, your time, your energy, your talents, your stuff.

Maybe the key to generosity is found in remembering who owns it all.

Read James 1:17. Who is the source of "every good and perfect gift" in your life? *Jesus*

How does it help you to be more generous when you know in your head and in your heart that everything you have comes from God? *Thankful — channel out like aquaduct.*

In what ways does fear keep you from being a more generous person? How can you change that?

How can greater thankfulness in your life move you toward greater generosity?

As we mentioned yesterday, Jesus' sacrifice on the cross is the ultimate example of generosity. We can never out give or repay the generosity on display through His sacrificial death.

How did Jesus' words and actions speak generosity to the people He encountered during His life on earth?

How does the cross stand as a stark reminder of Jesus' generosity toward us?

At the end of the Introduction for this week (p. 138), you wrote down the name of someone you considered to be a generous person. There's a good chance the person you hold in such high regard is not considered wealthy by the world's standards. They may not own houses and land, but they are full of the love of Christ. May that be said of us also. Let's remember we follow and serve a God who owns the cattle on a thousand hills (Ps. 50:10). In fact, He owns it all (Ps. 24:1) and freely gives to us according to His riches in glory (Phil. 4:19). May we reflect His heart as we establish our legacy of generosity.

IN YOUR OWN WORDS: How would you explain to someone else that generosity is about more than just money?

IN YOUR OWN LIFE: Following the Shunammite woman's example, where do you have opportunities to show generosity in your actions toward others?

DAY 3 LOYALTY: RUTH

The popular animated children's film *Toy Story* released in 1995 and featured a theme song titled "You've Got a Friend in Me." The song was nominated for an Academy Award for Best Original Song and the Golden Globe Award for Best Original Song.

In the *Toy Story* movie, this song reflects the sweet friendship between a boy and his toys, especially his beloved cowboy doll, Woody. The lyrics reflect the loyalty between the two—sticking together through good times and troubles.[88]

Loyalty is a highly valued commodity in family relationships, friendships, the workplace, and even on sports teams.

How would you define the word *loyalty*?

Someone has your back

What does loyalty look like in action?

Think about your own life. What's the greatest act of loyalty that you've experienced?

SET IN REBELLIOUS TIMES
When we look to the Bible for examples of loyalty, Ruth catches our eyes. Her story is found in a short book that bears her name. But Ruth stands tall as a model of loyalty, through her words and actions.

Ruth's story takes place during the time of the judges, a time of rebellion and disorder when "everyone did whatever seemed right to him" (Judg. 17:6) with little regard for God and His laws. Against the bigger timeline of the Bible, the period of the judges reached from the conquest of the land led by Joshua until David's rise as king. Bible scholars are uncertain of when the Book of Ruth was written, but they suggest the writing likely happened during or after King David's reign.

As we look into the story, we will see that Ruth and Naomi made hard decisions in the face of challenging circumstances.

When have you felt forced to make a hard decision because of a challenging circumstance?

THEN THE PLANS UNRAVELED
Read Ruth 1:1-5.

These early verses tell us that a man named Elimelech, his wife Naomi, and their two sons left their home in Bethlehem because of a famine and moved to the pagan land of Moab. What might have been intended as a short-term solution to famine turned into a long-term stay. Eventually, Elimelech died and his two sons married Moabite women named Orpah and Ruth. More time passed and Naomi's two sons also died, leaving Naomi with her two daughters-in-law.

When have your plans taken an unexpected turn?

How did you respond when your plans didn't go as expected?

HABITS OF LOYALTY

Read Ruth 1:6-14.

When news that the famine back home had eased, Naomi decided to return home to Bethlehem (she'd been in Moab ten years). Naomi blessed her daughters-in-law and encouraged them to return home and possibly remarry someday.

Naomi praised Orpah and Ruth for the kindness they had shown to her whole family (v. 8). Ruth's habits of loyalty and love had apparently been lived out over a long period of time.

How and where can you establish habits of loyalty and love? In your family? In your community?

What shape could these habits of loyalty take? What would they look like in action?

Following Naomi's urging, Orpah returned home to her people. But Ruth decided to stay with Naomi and head to Israel. Ruth "clung to" Naomi (v. 14)—the same word used to describe the marriage relationship in Genesis 2:24.

A BOLD DEMONSTRATION OF LOYALTY

Read Ruth 1:15-18.

In these powerful words of commitment, Ruth bound herself to Naomi in life and even until death. Even more striking, this woman from the pagan land of Moab committed herself to Naomi's God, Yahweh. The promise to die and be buried where Naomi lived was considered the greatest possible commitment in the culture of that time.

Write out Ruth's words of loyalty in verses 16-17 below:

Who in your life needs you to be like Ruth to them—loyal, faithful, committed? Explain.

THE FAMILY TREE

Cultivating a legacy of loyalty can have an impact across generations. We see the impact of Ruth's loyalty to Naomi when we look at some of the genealogies in the Bible. While our study of Ruth's loyalty to Naomi focused on the first chapter of the book, if you read the remaining three chapters, you'll find the rest of the story. After returning to Bethlehem with Naomi, Ruth met and married Boaz, a relative of Ruth's late father-in-law. Ruth and Boaz had a son named Obed.

Read Ruth 4:18-22. Who was Obed's grandson?

What appears to be simply a wonderful story of loyalty tucked away in the Old Testament was actually part of God's greater plan—for the people of Israel to have a king named David and for the world to have an even greater King, the King of kings.

Read Matthew 1:5-6.

In Matthew 1:1-16, we see a fuller listing of the genealogy of this family line. Ruth's son Obed is there, and he was King David's grandfather. But this list concludes with the birth of Jesus.

Isn't it like God to use the most unexpected people and the most surprising plans at times to bring about the work of His kingdom? The short story is that Ruth was loyal and faithful to Naomi during challenging circumstances. The long story is that God included Ruth—an outsider from Moab—as a part of the family line of King David and ultimately Jesus Christ.

When have you seen God work through unexpected people or surprising plans to bring about His purposes in your own life?

IN YOUR OWN WORDS: Reflecting on the story of Ruth, how would you define loyalty?

IN YOUR OWN LIFE: What next steps could you take toward building a legacy of loyalty?

DAY 4 LOYALTY: JONATHAN & DAVID

Jonathan and David—they could easily have been fierce rivals. Jonathan was the king's son. David would become the next king. One young man possessed the bloodline and rightful claim to the throne. The other young man was God's choice for the next king. So how did these two potential rivals become such close friends?

Loyalty was a huge factor.

> Do you think loyalty is viewed as outdated or impractical in our culture today? If so, why?

A COMMITTED LOYALTY

Read 1 Samuel 18:1-4.

This description of Jonathan and David is recorded in the biblical narrative right after the account of David defeating Goliath. You quickly get a sense of the love and loyalty between the two young men in verse 1: "Jonathan was bound to David in close friendship." Both had already demonstrated great courage as warriors—Jonathan in defeating the Philistines in battle and David in slaying the Philistine giant, Goliath. Either one of them alone was a strong and capable young man. Yet they must have seen the value in working to build a loyal relationship with each other. Their actions show they valued the "we" over the "I."

> In what ways did Jonathan demonstrate his loyalty to David in this passage?

This passage also tells us that Jonathan loved David "as much as he loved himself" (v. 1). That phrase can also be translated "as much as he loved his own life." The words imply selflessness and self-sacrifice. President Woodrow Wilson, in a 1916 address, stated:

> "Loyalty means nothing unless it has at its heart the absolute principle of self-sacrifice."[89]

What comes to mind when you think of …
Selflessness:

Self-sacrifice:

Here's how *Merriam-Webster* defines these words:

Selflessness: having no concern for self[90]

Self-sacrifice: sacrifice of oneself or one's interest for others or for a cause or ideal[91]

Both words carry the idea of putting the needs of others before your own. Some in our culture might view these characteristics in a negative light, or at the least as not-so-positive traits. Maybe the idea of selflessness is wrongly associated with being a human doormat. But in God's kingdom, traits like selflessness and self-sacrifice are highly valued.

Would you use either of these words—*selfless* or *self-sacrificing*—to describe yourself? Why or why not?

Why is it difficult to consistently live out these traits?

For all of us, our natural bent is to ourselves. Only with God's help can we truly put the needs of others ahead of our own.

Verse 3 tells us Jonathan sealed their friendship by making a covenant with David. In those days, a covenant was an oath-bound promise. We don't usually think of our family relationships and friendships today in terms of covenants in the way that they did in the ancient world. The Hebrew word used translated as "covenant" in verse 3 technically means "to cut a covenant" and refers to the two people making ritual sacrifices as part of their promise to each other. With the covenant described in verse 3, Jonathan also gave David gifts—his robe, tunic, sword, bow, and belt. With these gifts, the king's son was acknowledging David's royal role as the next king of Israel.

How is loyalty sometimes costly?

LOYALTY BUILT TO LAST

Sometimes being loyal means choosing the more challenging path over the easy road. Over time, King Saul grew jealous of David and gave the order to have him killed (1 Sam. 19:1-3). Ignoring his father's instructions, Jonathan instead warned David that Saul wanted him dead. Jonathan even devised a plan for David to go into hiding. In doing so, he made the difficult choice to stand against his father to try to protect his friend.

Jonathan then advocated for David before his father, reminding Saul of how David had faithfully served the king. In doing so, Jonathan was temporarily successful in talking his father down from his plan to have David killed (1 Sam. 19:4-7).

Jonathan and David's loyalty to each other was tested in this moment, and would be tested again by King Saul's jealous anger. Yet their loyalty withstood the pulls and strain of family jealousy.

What factors or circumstances might strain the loyalties you currently hold with family? With friends? With Christ?

How can you cultivate strong relationships built to withstand the test of time and challenges?

LOYALTY MULTIPLIED

David's loyalty to Jonathan extended even beyond Jonathan's death. In 2 Samuel 9:1, David raised the question, "Is there anyone remaining from the family of Saul I can show kindness to for Jonathan's sake?" The answer was that Jonathan had a son named Mephibosheth who was living in hiding. David found Mephibosheth, returned land to him that had belonged to his grandfather Saul, and invited him to eat at the king's table. David treated Jonathan's son like his own son.

Loyalty has a way of multiplying like that. David could have viewed Jonathan's son as a potential rival, seeking to gain the throne. Instead, reflecting his loyalty to Jonathan, David looked for ways to help Mephibosheth.

When have you seen the benefits of loyalty overflow into other relationships and other areas of your life?

Could there be situations where a person should not stay in a relationship simply for the sake of old loyalties? Explain.

How do you know when it's time to step back from a relationship? In what ways do you use God's Word as a guide for all your relationships?

Let's be clear, there perhaps are (or will be) relationships you need to step back from or end because they are not healthy or safe. Or perhaps your loyalty to Christ should supersede a relationship that draws you away from God and His purpose for you. At that point, health and spiritual priorities trump loyalty. Seek God's wisdom in these relationships and situations. You absolutely want to be a loyal family member and friend, but not at the expense of your health or your relationship with Jesus.

OUR LOYALTY EXAMPLE

Think about Jesus' life and the ways He modeled loyalty. Consider:

- His loyalty in His relationship with the disciples;

- His loyalty in His friendships with Mary, Martha, and Lazarus;

- His loyalty in following His Father's plan;

- His loyalty even to those who rejected Him.

How would you describe the loyalty Jesus displayed?

How has Jesus shown loyalty to you?

Are you currently leaving a legacy of loyalty? If so, how? If not, what needs to change for you to have a loyalty like that of Christ?

IN YOUR OWN WORDS: How would you describe the loyalty evident in Jonathan and David's relationship?

IN YOUR OWN LIFE: Where in your own life could you work toward that kind of loyalty in your relationships with family and friends?

DAY 5 **GENEROSITY & LOYALTY**

This week we've examined generosity from both ends of the economic ladder—one person with little, one person with much—in the stories of the widow with two coins and the Shunammite woman. We saw how God can use what we have in powerful ways when we make our hearts and our resources available to Him.

We've also explored loyalty in the family relationship with Ruth and Naomi and in a friendship with Jonathan and David. These stories showed us how God uses loyalty to bind people's hearts together in both comfortable and challenging times. We saw that the loyalty between two people can even overflow to bring blessings to others around them.

When we think about legacy characteristics like generosity or loyalty, we see the best versions of these ideals in the way God interacts with His people. God showed generosity and loyalty to us, even when we were far away from Him. His generosity and loyalty are an outflowing of His love for us.

Think of ways you've seen God at work in your life, and list some examples in the space below:

I've seen God's generosity expressed in my life through ...

I've seen God's loyalty expressed in my life through ...

When we are more aware of how our lives are blessed because of God's generosity and loyalty, then a natural next step is to look for ways to touch the lives of those around us with the overflow of that generosity and loyalty.

LIVE GENEROUSLY

Try starting each day thanking God for His generosity toward you. Like water flowing downstream, generosity flows easily out of a thankful heart. So begin the day with the proper heart attitude of thankfulness for all God's good gifts, and then look for opportunities to live generously. Remind yourself that generosity is not just about dollars and cents. Generosity is also reflected in how we use our time, energy, resources, and talents.

Where could you make a difference this coming week through your generosity?

Where will you look for fresh opportunities to live generously, building a legacy of generosity in the days ahead?

WEAR LOYALTY LIKE A NECKLACE

The Book of Proverbs is a helpful "life manual" concerning our relationships with each other and with God. Proverbs 3:3 teaches us,

"Never let loyalty and faithfulness leave you.
Tie them around your neck; write them on the tablet of
your heart."

This is such a great reminder that so many of these legacy qualities are not just things we pick up or discard based on our own convenience or comfort. Rather these legacy qualities—like loyalty—should be evident in our lifestyle and reflected in our heart attitudes. As you go through the day, picture yourself wearing loyalty like a necklace, so that your family members and friends are blessed by that loyalty on display in your life.

What steps could you take right now to write loyalty "on the tablet of your heart"?

In what ways might others around you see that loyalty in your words and actions?

Commit the following Scripture verses to memory to help develop the godly characteristics of generosity and loyalty.

"Freely you received, freely give."
MATTHEW 10:8

"Never let loyalty and faithfulness leave you. Tie them around your neck; write them on the tablet of your heart."
PROVERBS 3:3

session six:

WISDOM & TEACHING

WATCH

To watch the free video of Session Six, go to LifeWay.com/LegacyStudy.

DISCUSS

What is one thing that stood out to you from the video?

What's the difference between wisdom and knowledge?

Would you consider yourself a wise person? Explain.

What opportunities do you have to teach?

How are you currently teaching those younger than you the ways of God?

How do wisdom and teaching contribute to leaving a legacy worth following?

INTRODUCTION

"Wisdom is the right use of knowledge. To know is not to be wise. Many men know a great deal, and are all the greater fools for it. There is no fool so great a fool as a knowing fool. But to know how to use knowledge is to have wisdom."[92]

CHARLES SPURGEON

A research team at University of California, San Diego conducted a study aimed at measuring people's wisdom.

These researchers in the School of Medicine created a tool that helps them determine a person's wisdom. They call the tool SD-WISE (San Diego Wisdom Scale).[93] The research team tested their tool on more than five hundred adults ranging in age from twenty-five to forty. The tool measured things like people's empathy, social cooperation, emotional regulation, self-understanding, tolerance of diverse values, and the ability to deal with uncertainty in life—factors that help the researchers assess a person's wisdom. The people taking part in the study answered a series of questions. Then the research team reviewed their responses to the questions and determined each person's degree of wisdom.

While our definitions of wisdom might vary, it's likely all of us have someone in our lives we would describe as wise.

Who do you know who displays wisdom? How do you see evidence of wisdom in that person's life?

Scripture gives us a great understanding of wisdom. We can read how wisdom is described as a highly valued quality, and we can see how wisdom affects people's lives, both the blessings when it is applied and the consequences when it is not.

As you grow in wisdom and knowledge, it's your responsibility to pass those down to the generations that follow. Though you may not call yourself a teacher, or stand in a classroom full of students, you will have opportunities to mentor and guide those who come behind you. It may be over coffee or around your kitchen table, on a park bench or a church pew. Whatever the moment and time, teach. So many need to know what God has taught you and brought you through. Your experience with Him and knowledge of Him are invaluable to those following in your steps.

DAY 1 **WISDOM: DEBORAH**

In Judges 4, we find the story of Deborah, a judge and a prophetess in Israel around 1200 BC. The period of the judges, a period of about three hundred years, is marked by increasing disobedience against God and the increase in pagan worship practices. The last verse of the Book of Judges sums up the spiritual condition of the people.

> "In those days there was no king in Israel;
> everyone did whatever seemed right to him."
> **JUDGES 21:25**

The word for "judges" can also be translated "governors." The judges governed and also provided spiritual leadership to the people of Israel. (Although, there were some ungodly judges.)

CYCLE OF SIN

Read Judges 4:1-5. What hints do we get from these verses about the Israelites' behavior during the time Deborah ruled in Israel?

In these early verses of chapter 4 we see the destructive sin cycle that appears throughout the book. In verse 1, the key word is "again."

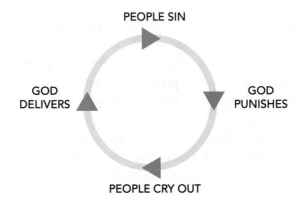

Have you ever experienced this kind of cycle in your life? Explain.

At this time, a Canaanite king named Jabin oppressed the people of Israel. The commander of his army was named Sisera.

A UNIQUE LEADER

Verse 4 tell us that Deborah, wife of Lappidoth, was both a prophetess and a judge. As her story unfolds, we will also see she was a military leader. Besides Deborah, only two other people in the Bible held this unique combination of offices—prophet, judge, military leader—and those two people were Moses and Samuel.[94] Pretty elite company!

We find one of the first clues to Deborah's wisdom in verse 5, where it tells us that the people of Israel came to her "to settle disputes."

Who would you turn to if you needed help settling an
argument or resolving a dispute?
□ a family member
□ a trusted friend
□ a pastor or counselor
□ a teacher or coach
□ other person:

What is it about that person that makes you want to
seek out their advice?

INTRODUCING BARAK

Read Judges 4:6-10.

As the story of Deborah continues, we find her giving instructions to
a man named Barak. She was sending Barak into battle to fight against
Sisera, the commander of the Canaanite army. She assured Barak that
God would give him the victory over their enemies.

Barak's name means "lightning," but how is his
response to Deborah's instructions unlike lightning?

Wisely knowing that this was God's plan, Deborah agreed to go with
Barak. There at Kedesh, Barak successfully led an army of ten thousand.

SISERA AND HIS IRON CHARIOTS

Read Judges 4:11-16.

When Sisera heard that Barak had gathered troops, the commander
reacted with a show of force by summoning his nine hundred chariots

and his infantry to the Wadi Kishon, the place where God said the battle would take place.

From a human standpoint, Sisera's army and his nine hundred iron chariots had the clear advantage. They had greater firepower, and the morale of the people of Israel had to be low, having been "harshly oppressed" by Sisera for twenty years (v. 3). But while Sisera put his faith in iron chariots, Deborah put her faith in God.

Have there been moments when following God's plan felt like a disadvantage in your life? Explain.

When or how have you seen God's plan—God's wisdom—be the best plan for your life?

Deborah continued to speak God's wisdom to Barak, instructing him to move his army forward to battle. Note her question to Barak: "Hasn't the LORD gone before you?" (v. 14).

How does it change your outlook on life to know God has gone before you in every step you take?

Keeping His promise, God threw Sisera, his army, and his chariots "into a panic" (v. 15). Barak defeated Sisera's army and his iron chariots—and "not a single man was left" (v. 16).

What evidence do we see that Deborah listened to God and followed His leadership?

What qualities do you think made Deborah a wise leader?

SINGING GOD'S PRAISES

If we look ahead to Judges 5:1-15, we find Deborah's song following their victory in battle over Sisera.

Who does Deborah credit with her success in battle?

Deborah had every reason to be proud of her accomplishments as a judge, a prophet, and a military leader. Yet she was wise to realize that ultimately, her success came from God. Recognizing God's part in our achievements is an important step toward wisdom.

In fact, we can gain more wisdom not only by recognizing God's presence and work, but also by requesting wisdom from Him.

Read James 1:5. How can we acquire godly wisdom? And how does God respond to our requests?

WISDOM NUGGETS IN PROVERBS

Much of the wisdom we seek from God comes from His Word. It is a great resource for discovering what godly wisdom looks and acts like.

Take a look at these verses—Proverbs 1:7; 2:6; 3:5-7; 4:6-7,20-27—and jot down in the space below what you discover about wisdom.

Godly wisdom is not just reserved for the spiritual elite or for great spiritual leaders. It is available to all of us.

IN YOUR OWN WORDS: After this study, how would you define wisdom?

IN YOUR OWN LIFE: What events are happening in your life right now where you could apply godly wisdom?

DAY 2 **WISDOM: ABIGAIL**

In the Old Testament book of 1 Samuel we find an interesting pair of opposites—the wife and husband, Abigail and Nabal. Chapter 25 presents us with a character study of the wisdom of Abigail. Her wise ways stand in sharp contrast to her husband, Nabal, the "worthless fool" (v. 17). Abigail demonstrated what godly wisdom in action looks like when she faced extremely challenging circumstances.

> Read 1 Samuel 25:1-8. What do we find out about Abigail and Nabal in these verses?

Abigail and Nabal are part of a larger story about David and his six hundred men who were hiding in the Wilderness of Paran. The wealthy landowner, Nabal, was shearing his sheep, a festive event since wool was a valuable commodity. David and his men had protected Nabal's shepherds and livestock as they moved about in the wilderness areas (vv. 15-16). Now David asked Nabal if they could have food to eat from the sheep shearing celebration. This was not an unreasonable request. It even gave Nabal an opportunity to show his gratitude for the protection David and his men had provided. But remember Scripture's earlier description of Nabal—a man who was "harsh and evil in his dealings" (v. 3). He was not a man known for his gratitude.

FOOLISHNESS MEETS ANGER

> Read 1 Samuel 25:9-17. How did Nabal react to the visit from David's men asking for food?

Notice Nabal's insulting response—he compared David to a runaway slave hiding from King Saul (v. 10). When David heard how Nabal had responded to his request, he and his men armed themselves with swords and planned an attack on the fool.

These two men—one rude (Nabal), the other angry (David)—were not a good combination. But one of Nabal's young men realized the foolishness in the way Nabal had treated David, so he went to tell Abigail what had happened. The man reminded Abigail of all the good David and his men had done in protecting Nabal's shepherds and the livestock. Look at verse 17 and note the way the young man pleaded with Abigail to intervene. The young man's words suggest that this was probably not the first time Nabal had demonstrated such foolish behavior (and perhaps not the first time Abigail needed to respond in wisdom to right the situation).

Sometimes—but maybe not all the time—the wise person needs to step in and help correct the mess someone else has created.

How do you decide when to get involved in fixing a situation?

How do you decide when to step back?

A SWIFT MOVE TOWARD REPAIR
Read 1 Samuel 25:18-22.

Once Abigail heard the story of Nabal's insulting behavior toward David, she took action.

How did Abigail act with wisdom to defuse the
situation?

Abigail arrived just in time to hear David describe the harsh revenge
he planned to inflict on Nabal and all his men. David had protected
Nabal's shepherds and sheep "for nothing," he said, and Nabal had paid
him back "evil for good" (v. 21). David was justified in his anger toward
Nabal, and he wanted to get even. But getting even is not the biblical
way of dealing with people who have wronged you (Rom. 12:9-21;
1 Pet. 3:8-9).

How can you act in wisdom when someone wrongs you?

WORDS AND ACTIONS WISELY CHOSEN
Read 1 Samuel 25:23-31.

Notice Abigail's swift move from riding on the donkey to kneeling with
her face to the ground in front of David, showing him honor. She told
David that she bore the guilt of the way Nabal had treated him. Abigail
begged David to forget about Nabal and his foolish actions. She offered
him the gift of food, and asked for David's forgiveness. Then, looking to
the future, Abigail spoke of the lasting dynasty that would come from
David's family line. She saw the day when God would appoint David
ruler over Israel, and she did not want David to carry the weight of
a "troubled conscience" at that time, regretting any past actions
regarding Nabal (v. 31). Abigail's final words were an appeal to David
to remember her.

Instead of reacting to the emotions in the moment, Abigail looked at the
big picture and chose her words and actions based on God's best plan
for David's life.

How did Abigail display wisdom in her words and actions?

How can keeping the big picture in mind help you act with wisdom, especially when emotions are high?

How might her wise words have encouraged David's faith?

How can your wise words and actions encourage the faith of those around you?

"RIGHT USE OF KNOWLEDGE"
Go back to the Introduction of this session (p. 167) and read the Charles Spurgeon quote again.

Read 1 Samuel 25:32-35. What was the result of Abigail showing "right use of knowledge" in her wise actions?

How has someone's wisdom kept you from making a bad decision?

In just a short time, David moved from planning to kill Nabal and all his men to leaving in peace. David spoke words of blessing to God, to Abigail's discernment, and to Abigail. David recognized God's hand in sending Abigail to prevent him from seeking revenge against Nabal.

Abigail's swift, wise actions prevented a disaster that could have had severe repercussions. She truly left a legacy of wisdom. Perhaps you're facing your own showdown created by someone else or of your own making. Or maybe you're just dealing with the everyday decisions of life. Both will have future impact. Act with wisdom. Know that the words and actions you take will go a long way in establishing a godly legacy of wisdom.

IN YOUR OWN WORDS: After your study of Abigail, what might you add to your definition of wisdom?

IN YOUR OWN LIFE: Look at your calendar or planner for the days ahead—what upcoming events could benefit from your application of godly wisdom through your words and actions?

DAY 3 **TEACHING: HULDAH**

Most of us can recall at least one teacher who made a significant impact at a pivotal point in our lives. Bill Gates recalls one such teacher. Gates, who is probably most famous for founding the Microsoft Corporation, says that Blanche Caffiere, "a very kindly librarian and teacher," had a huge influence in his life.[95]

When Gates met Mrs. Caffiere, he was a fourth-grade-boy with "atrocious handwriting ... and a comically messy desk." Gates also liked to read. "Mrs. Caffiere took me under her wing," Gates said, "and helped make it okay for me to be a messy, nerdy boy who was reading lots of books."[96] Reflecting on her influence, Gates noted, "She pulled me out of my shell by sharing her love of books." She asked Gates questions about what he was interested in and then found books for him that targeted his specific interests. "Once I'd read them," he said, "she would make the time to discuss them with me. 'Did you like it?' she would ask. 'Why? What did you learn?' She genuinely listened to what I had to say."[97]

Gates' relationship with Mrs. Caffiere, the librarian and teacher, shaped the boy he was then and the man he is today—his first large-scale effort in philanthropy involved libraries.

> Who was or is a significant teacher in your life? What did you learn from that person?

A TEACHER AND A KING
In 2 Kings 22 (and also in 2 Chronicles 34), we find the story of Huldah, a woman who played a significant role as a teacher to King Josiah.

The Bible tells us that as king, Josiah "did what was right in the LORD's sight and walked in all the ways of his ancestor David; he did not turn to the right or the left" (2 Kings 22:2). However, that was not the case for many of the kings who preceded Josiah. They did evil, leading the people into idolatry and other pagan worship practices.

During his reign, King Josiah decided to repair the temple. While the construction was taking place, workers discovered the book of the law. When it was read in his presence, Josiah was so moved that he tore his clothes in grief, realizing that the people had "not obeyed the words of this book" (v. 13).

Read 2 Kings 22:14.

As king, Josiah wielded great power. Yet he recognized he needed help in understanding the book of the law. So the royal officials sought out Huldah to instruct them on studying and obeying God's Word.

Huldah is described as a prophetess. She is not the only female prophet named in the Old Testament. Miriam, Moses' sister, and Deborah, one of the judges, are also named as prophetesses.

Why are teachers of God's Word so important in our faith walk?

Who has helped you better understand and apply God's Word?

Notice that even though he was surrounded by pagan worship, King Josiah took the bold steps of seeking out a teacher who could help him understand God's Word. He found one in Huldah, a teacher who had not crumbled under the weight of the idol worship and sinful behavior among the people. She had remained faithful to God.

Do you ever find it difficult to stay true to God's Word in a culture that continues to compromise and defy it? Explain.

How can you remain teachable regarding the things of God, even as you mature in age?

DISOBEDIENCE BRINGS PUNISHMENT
Read 2 Kings 22:15-20.

Huldah's message was true, but hard to hear. She explained that God would bring judgment on the people because they had abandoned Him "and burned incense to other gods" (v. 17). The people of Judah would feel the crushing weight of God's wrath because of their sinful disobedience.

Huldah sent a different message to King Josiah. Review verses 18-20. Why and how would Josiah be spared God's punishment?

In a culture where God was not respected and people chased after disobedience, Huldah stood out as a teacher who pursued the truth of God's Word and was unashamed to teach it to others—even to the powerful king.

What opportunities is God giving you to teach others about what you have learned in your faith walk?

Are you stepping forward in obedience to teach others about Him? Explain.

If not, what steps do you need to take to be a faithful teacher of God, His Word, and His ways?

TEACHING ... EXPANDED

Search the verses below to uncover more of what the Bible says about teaching.

Fill in the blanks with the information you find in the verses:

1. Deuteronomy 32:2: Our teaching should be like

   _____.

2. Matthew 5:19: Those who teach God's commands to others are called _____ in the kingdom of heaven.

3. Romans 12:6-7: Teaching is just one of many different _____ given to believers.

4. Colossians 3:16: One way to teach others is through _____, _____, and _____ _____.

5. Titus 2:7: Our teaching should reflect _____ and

   _____.

Huldah was called upon to teach the truth, to share a difficult message. And she did. She was faithful to the truth of God's Word. We need to be grateful to those who have been faithful to share God's Word with us, even when the message was difficult to share and difficult to receive. But we also need to understand the responsibility of being one who teaches the truth of God. That could be teaching the story of Scripture to six year olds every Sunday, mentoring a friend one-on-one, or imparting biblical wisdom to your teenager. Teaching can take many forms, but we must be willing to leave that kind of legacy behind.

IN YOUR OWN WORDS: How would you explain the importance of the legacy of teaching?

IN YOUR OWN LIFE: Who do you need to be a teacher to today, helping them understand the truth about God, His Word, and His ways?

DAY 4 TEACHING: LOIS & EUNICE

Who was your favorite school teacher? What was it that made this person your favorite?

When we think of teachers who impacted our lives in significant ways, our thoughts usually turn to classroom teachers from our school days. But for many of us, the earliest teachers we had were in the home—parents, grandparents, aunts, and uncles. Timothy benefited in this way.

Timothy played an important role in the New Testament. He traveled with Paul and was also sent out by Paul on a number of mission trips. In six of the New Testament letters that Paul authored, he named Timothy as a coauthor. Paul even addressed two of his letters to Timothy. And near the end of his life, when death was near, Paul called for Timothy to come and be with him.

So how did this man, who was so important in Paul's life and who played such a significant role in the New Testament we have today, come to be the man he was? The Book of 2 Timothy holds some clues. In Paul's second letter to Timothy we find a beautiful glimpse of the teaching that can be so powerful within the family relationships.

THANKS TO THE TEACHERS
Read 2 Timothy 1:4-5.

Paul opened this letter to Timothy with words of thanksgiving. And part of Paul's thankfulness touched on the heritage of faith that Timothy received. Paul commended Timothy's grandmother Lois and his mother Eunice, highlighting a legacy of faith across three generations. This legacy of faith was watered and tended like a garden through the teaching poured into Timothy's life.

How did Paul describe the evidence of faithful teaching
in Timothy's family?

Paul saw Timothy's faith as proof of the faith in these women who
played such an important part in nurturing and teaching Timothy.

Who was the first person to teach you about the faith?

How did this person's teaching lay the spiritual
foundation for your faith, and how has it impacted
where your spiritual life is today?

It's evident that Lois and Eunice laid the groundwork for Timothy's
spiritual life. It's unlikely that Lois and Eunice were trained educators.
Likely, they were just two women who loved God, loved Timothy, and
realized how important it was to pass their faith along to him.

NURTURE A CHILD-LIKE FAITH
Read 2 Timothy 3:14-17.

Paul called attention to Timothy's faith again in chapter 3. He told
Timothy to keep growing "in what you have learned and firmly believed"
(v. 14). Paul praised those who had taught him from infancy, likely
referring again to Lois and Eunice. And it's important to note that what
Timothy learned from infancy was "the sacred Scriptures" (v. 15).
The faith Paul saw evidence of and praised in Timothy had its begin-
nings in the fertile heart of a young child, nurtured through the
teaching of his mother and grandmother.

What do these verses reveal about the importance of godly, biblical teachers in the lives of preschool and school-age children?

Maybe you come from a family where biblical faith was not lived or taught. If that's the case, take a moment to thank God for the people He put in your life who did teach you about Him and His Word. Also, realize you have the opportunity to start that legacy of godly teaching in your family today. All it takes is one person willing to share God's Word with the next generation for a legacy of godly teaching to blossom and grow.

HELP WANTED: TEACHERS

You may think there's no way you're qualified to teach the Bible. Review today's passages from 2 Timothy and note that Paul does not list Lois and Eunice's qualifications for teaching. He simply praised them for the work they did in Timothy's life from the time he was very young.

Check the qualifications you think a person needs in order to be a godly teacher:
- □ a seminary degree
- □ a love for God
- □ a lot of free time
- □ a love for God's Word
- □ a thankfulness for what God has done for you
- □ experience as a trained school teacher
- □ a willingness to serve God and others
- □ other qualifications:

It doesn't take a seminary degree to pass the faith along to the next generation. A heart for God and a love for His Word quickly set you on that path. Remember, if you know Christ, you have the Holy Spirit within you. And one of the Spirit's jobs is to teach you the truth (John 14:26) as you personally study and place yourself under solid biblical teaching.

LAYING UP GOD'S WORD IN OUR HEARTS

We also find words in the Old Testament that help us better understand how God intends His Word to be passed down. The following verses capture Moses speaking God's instruction to the people of Israel.

Read Deuteronomy 11:18-21 below. Underline the phrases in these verses that describe where and how the teaching of God's Word was to take place:

"Imprint these words of mine on your hearts and minds, bind them as a sign on your hands, and let them be a symbol on your foreheads. Teach them to your children, talking about them when you sit in your house and when you walk along the road, when you lie down and when you get up. Write them on the doorposts of your house and on your city gates, so that as long as the heavens are above the earth, your days and those of your children may be many in the land the LORD swore to give your fathers."

DEUTERONOMY 11:18-21

According to Moses, how and where is the teaching to take place?

Is this currently taking place in your home and family? Explain.

How can you play a role in helping others to "imprint these words of mine in your hearts and in your minds"? **With your children?**

With your grandchildren?

With other young people in your church family or community?

Notice how these verses emphasize that teaching God's Word to future generations is not a one-time event or even a once-a-week event. Moses' words paint a picture of a consistent, on-going relationship between teacher and child. Teaching the faith is to be a part of your lifestyle. That seems to be what took place in Timothy's home and family. And that's what needs to take place in yours as you leave a legacy of teaching.

IN YOUR OWN WORDS: How has this week of study helped you understand the legacy of teaching?

IN YOUR OWN LIFE: Who do you know—children, grandchildren, nieces, nephews, teenagers in your church family—who could benefit from your teaching today? What steps will you take toward investing in those peoples' lives?

DAY 5 **WISDOM & TEACHING**

This week we've looked at wisdom through the lens of two Old Testament stories—Deborah leading her people and Abigail repairing a disastrous situation involving a future king. Both of these women acted with wisdom to advance the purpose of God.

The Bible tells us over and over again that God is the source of true wisdom. And this godly wisdom we seek for our own lives is never meant to be hoarded—we are to share God's wisdom through teaching it to others.

> How have you applied God's wisdom to a situation in your life?

> How have you helped someone else through a decision or difficult time by sharing God's wisdom?

Seeking God's wisdom daily, in every situation we face, better prepares us to share that wisdom in teachable moments with others who need to know of God's love and power in their lives.

SEEK HIS WISDOM

When you try to turn your heart toward God's wisdom, perhaps it feels like a far-off, unattainable goal. Maybe Satan brings to mind all the not-so-smart, reckless, rash, unwise decisions you've ever made. Don't listen to the voice that tries to dredge up past mistakes. God is fully able to forgive the things in our past. And He is never, ever stingy with His wisdom. Remember what James 1:5 teaches us:

> "Now if any of you lacks wisdom, he should ask God—who gives to all generously and ungrudgingly—and it will be given to him."

Underline the word "generously" in the middle of the verse. God does not hide or withhold His wisdom. He doesn't say that only perfect people have access to His wisdom. God gives His wisdom to us generously—all we have to do is ask.

TOUCH LIVES THROUGH TEACHING

This week we've also discussed the legacy of teaching by studying the Old Testament character Huldah, who taught a king, and the New Testament family pair of Lois and Eunice, whose teaching encouraged Timothy to grow strong in his faith. We saw how God used ordinary people—a prophetess, a grandmother, a mother—to teach others the importance of obeying God and having a strong faith in Him.

Spend a moment thanking God for the teachers He has brought into your life; people who have nurtured, encouraged, and challenged you as you've grown in your faith.

Take a moment to think about people you know with whom you could share words of nurture, encouragement, or challenge to encourage their faith. Jot down their names below. Ask God to give you the wisdom and the opportunity to help build their faith, in the ways Huldah, Lois, and Eunice helped build the faith of those around them.

Commit the following Scripture verses to memory to help you leave a legacy of wisdom and teaching.

"Now if any of you lacks wisdom, he should ask God—who gives to all generously and ungrudgingly—and it will be given to him."
JAMES 1:5

"We proclaim him, warning and teaching everyone with all wisdom, so that we may present everyone mature in Christ. I labor for this, striving with his strength that works powerfully in me."
COLOSSIANS 1:28-29

LEGACY LEADER GUIDE

A WORD TO THE LEADER

Thanks for stepping up to take on the responsibility and blessing of leading your group through this Bible study! The following tips and information will help you guide the study.

GROUP SESSIONS

Each group session contains the following elements:

GATHER: This is a time to greet and welcome everyone, and get conversation started. In the first session, you're provided with some icebreaker questions. In the subsequent sessions, there will be a list of questions to help participants review the previous week's personal study. Please note that because the video portion of the study is optional and you may not choose to use it, we've provided a substantial list of questions for discussion. Feel free to adapt, skip, or add questions according to the needs of your group.

WATCH (optional): Free videos are provided online at Lifeway.com/ LegacyStudy. These videos feature Jackie Green and Lauren Green McAfee using illustrations and sharing personal stories to introduce each week of the study. Each video session was filmed at the Museum of the Bible in Washington, D.C., and highlights several areas of the museum. If you choose to use the videos, encourage participants to take notes on the Watch pages in their Bible study books.

DISCUSS (optional): If you use the videos, we've provided a list of questions on each session's Discuss page to help your group debrief what they heard in the video teaching. Again, feel free to adapt, skip, or add questions as needed to foster discussion.

PERSONAL STUDY

Each session contains five days of personal study to help participants dig into God's Word for themselves.

PREPARE

STUDY: After your group has met for Session One, make sure you've completed each week's personal study before the subsequent group sessions. Review the opening questions, and consider how best to lead your group through this time. If you're using the videos, you'll also want to review each session and look over the discussion questions that follow.

PRAY: Set aside time each week to pray for yourself and each member of your group.

CONNECT: Find ways to interact and stay engaged with each member of your group throughout the study. Make use of social media, email, and handwritten notes to encourage them. Continue these connections even after the study ends.

NOTE: There is no Session Seven video, but we have provided some questions to use for an optional Session Seven to give you the opportunity to debrief what you studied in Session Six.

GATHER

Welcome your group to the study and distribute Bible study books to each participant. Encourage discussion by asking the following questions:

- What drew you to this Bible study?
- When you hear the word *legacy* what comes to mind?
- Do you think about the legacy you're leaving behind?
- Who is someone you know who has left or is leaving a great legacy? How so?
- Why is it important to leave a legacy worth following?

WATCH (OPTIONAL)

To watch the free video of Session One, go to LifeWay.com/LegacyStudy. Encourage participants to take notes or jot down questions on the Watch page.

DISCUSS (OPTIONAL)

Use the questions found on page 8 to debrief the video.

GATHER

Welcome your group back to the study. Use the following questions to review Session One personal study.

- What day of personal study was the most meaningful to you? Why?
- When was a time you wrestled between fear and courage? Which did you choose, and what was the tipping point?
- What about Esther's story inspires you?
- How has God positioned you where you are in life "for such a time as this"? What people are depending on your courage?
- How would you define "comfort zone"? How easily do you move outside of yours?
- Is God currently asking you to take courageous steps outside of your comfort zone? Explain.
- What about Mary's story inspires you?
- When have you seen God accomplish what you knew to be humanly impossible?
- How has God proven to you that you can trust Him implicitly?
- Why is it important that you leave a legacy of courage and faith? How are you currently building that kind of legacy?

WATCH (OPTIONAL)

To watch the free video of Session Two, go to LifeWay.com/LegacyStudy. Encourage participants to take notes or jot down questions on the Watch page.

DISCUSS (OPTIONAL)

Use the questions found on page 40 to debrief the video.

GATHER

Welcome your group back to the study. Use the following questions to review Session Two personal study.

- What day of personal study was the most meaningful to you? Why?
- What is the boldest thing you've ever done? What inspired you to do it?
- What about the story of the woman at the well inspires you?
- When has God challenged you to seize opportunities greater than what you were reaching for? How did you respond?
- When has time with Jesus changed your perspective on a problem or situation and given you new boldness?
- What about Mary Magdalene's story inspires you?
- Share about your encounter with Jesus that led you to receive Him as Lord and Savior.
- What does it mean to have a divine appointment? When have you experienced such a moment?
- Identify one person God has placed in your path to hear your witness of Christ. How can you run after that person?
- Why is it important that you leave a legacy of boldness and witness? How are you currently building that kind of legacy?

WATCH (OPTIONAL)

To watch the free video of Session Three, go to LifeWay.com/LegacyStudy. Encourage participants to take notes or jot down questions on the Watch page.

DISCUSS (OPTIONAL)

Use the questions found on page 74 to debrief the video.

GATHER

Welcome your group back to the study. Use the following questions to review Session Three personal study.

- What day of personal study was the most meaningful to you? Why?
- Who is the most compassionate person you know?
- What did you learn about compassion through Pharaoh's daughter rescuing Moses?
- Why is action a necessary part of compassion?
- How might risk be involved in showing compassion to someone?
- Is it possible for us to show the same kind of compassion that Jesus expressed? Explain.
- How does Jehosheba's action inspire you to leave a legacy of rescue?
- Who in your current sphere of influence needs to be rescued? What steps are you taking to provide that rescue?
- Most of us quickly agree that God uses unlikely people all the time, but too many of us never include ourselves in that group. Why? What do you think disqualifies you from being used by God?
- Why is it important that you leave a legacy of compassion and rescue? How are you currently building that kind of legacy?

WATCH (OPTIONAL)

To watch the free video of Session Four, go to LifeWay.com/LegacyStudy. Encourage participants to take notes or jot down questions on the Watch page.

DISCUSS (OPTIONAL)

Use the questions found on page 104 to debrief the video.

GATHER

Welcome your group back to the study. Use the following questions to review Session Four personal study.

- What day of personal study was the most meaningful to you? Why?
- When have you seen God powerfully answer prayer in your life or someone else's?
- What did you learn about prayer from Hannah's story?
- What's one prayer you've prayed that you're glad God didn't answer the way you wanted Him to?
- Explain this statement: Prayer is about discovering God's will and not about getting Him to do ours.
- Why is tenacity important to our spiritual lives?
- What do you learn about tenacity from the Syrophoenician woman?
- When does great faith keep asking and when does great faith accept God has a better way than what I want?
- What does the phrase "finish well" mean to you? How do you apply that to your spiritual life?
- Why is it important that you leave a legacy of prayer and tenacity? How are you currently building that kind of legacy?

WATCH (OPTIONAL)

To watch the free video of Session Five, go to LifeWay.com/LegacyStudy. Encourage participants to take notes or jot down questions on the Watch page.

DISCUSS (OPTIONAL)

Use the questions found on page 136 to debrief the video.

GATHER

Welcome your group back to the study. Use the following questions to review Session Five personal study.

- What day of personal study was the most meaningful to you? Why?
- When you think of a generous person, who comes to mind? Why? How does this person display generosity?
- What do you learn about generosity from the poor widow and the Shunammite woman?
- In what other ways could you be generous besides giving your money?
- In what ways can fear keep you from being a more generous person? How can you change that?
- What's the greatest act of loyalty that you've experienced?
- What did you learn about loyalty from Ruth's story?
- Who in your life needs you to be like Ruth to them—loyal, faithful, committed? Explain.
- How can you cultivate strong relationships built to withstand the test of time and challenges?
- Why is it important that you leave a legacy of generosity and loyalty? How are you currently building that kind of legacy?

WATCH (OPTIONAL)

To watch the free video of Session Six, go to LifeWay.com/LegacyStudy. Encourage participants to take notes or jot down questions on the Watch page.

DISCUSS (OPTIONAL)

Use the questions found on page 166 to debrief the video.

GATHER

Welcome your group back to the study. Use the following questions to review Session Six personal study.

- What day of personal study was the most meaningful to you? Why?
- Who is the wisest person you know? How do you see this person displaying wisdom?
- What do you learn about wisdom from the stories of Deborah and Abigail?
- How can keeping the big picture in mind help you act with wisdom?
- To what current life situation do you need to apply the wisdom of God?
- Why are teachers of God's Word so important in your faith walk?
- How do you see the importance of a legacy of teaching through the actions of Huldah, Lois, and Eunice?
- What opportunities is God giving you to teach others about what you have learned in your faith walk? How are you responding to those opportunities?
- Why is it important that you leave a legacy of wisdom and teaching? How are you currently building that kind of legacy?
- What are three significant things you'll take away from this study?
- Do you really believe that one ordinary life can make an eternal difference? How have you already seen that happen in your life?
- What changes will you make in the coming days to better live a life of legacy?

ENDNOTES

SESSION ONE

1 Charles Studd. "Only One Life." Reddit. com. https://www.reddit.com/r/TrueChristian/comments/4n15n5/only_one_life_twill_soon_be_past_poem_by_c_t_stud/ (accessed March 18, 2019).

2 Elisabeth Elliot, *A Chance to Die* (Old Tapan, NJ: Revell, 1987), 117.

3 The Traveling Team. "History of Mission: Elisabeth Elliot & Rachel Saint." TheTravelingTeam.org. http://www.thetravelingteam.org/articles/elisabeth-elliot-rachel-saint (accessed February 21, 2019).

4 *Ibid.*

5 Elisabeth Elliot, "About Elisabeth." Elisabethelliot.org. http://www.elisabethelliot.org/about.html (accessed February 21, 2019).

6 Mervin Breneman, *The New American Commentary*, vol. 10, *Ezra, Nehemiah, Esther* (Nashville, TN: Broadman & Holman, 1993).

7 *Ibid.*

8 Katherine Weber, "Rick Warren: Why God Encourages Christians to 'Fear Not' 365 Times in the Bible." ChristianPost. com. https://www.christianpost.com/news/rick-warren-why-god-encourages-christians-to-fear-not-365-times-in-the-bible-163029/ (accessed February 15, 2019).

9 John A. Shedd, *Salt from My Attic* (Portland, ME: Mosher Press, 1928).

10 Melanie Greenberg, "The Six Attributes of Courage." PsychologyToday.com. https://www.psychologytoday.com/us/blog/the-mindful-self-express/201208/the-six-attributes-courage (accessed February 16, 2019).

11 Karen H. Jobes, *Esther: The NIV Application Commentary* (Grand Rapids, MI: Zondervan, 1999), 212.

12 Marcus Tullius Cicero, *Cicero: Complete Works*, trans. C.D. Yonge (Hastings, East Sussex, UK: Delphi Classics, 2014).

13 Anne Ju. "Courage is the most important virtue, says writer and civil rights activist Maya Angelou at Convocation." News.cornell.edu. http://news.cornell.edu/stories/2008/05/courage-most-important-virtue-maya-angelou-tells-seniors (accessed February 16, 2019).

14 *Ibid.*, 244.

15 Brennan Manning, *Ruthless Trust: The Ragamuffin's Path to God* (San Francisco, CA: HarperSanFrancisco, 2000), 3.

16 Philip W. Comfort and Dan Lins, eds., *Life Application New Testament Commentary* (Carol Stream, IL: Tyndale, 2001).

17 *Ibid.*

18 Gerald L. Borchert, *The New American Commentary*, vol. 25a, *John 1-11* (Nashville, TN: Broadman & Holman, 1996).

19 Comfort and Lins, eds., *Life Application New Testament Commentary*.

20 Jerry Bridges, *Trusting God, Even When Life Hurts* (Colorado Springs, CO: NavPress, 1988).

21 William Peterson and Ardythe Peterson, *The Complete Book of Hymns* (Carol Stream, IL: Tyndale, 2006), 113.

22 Louisa Stead. "'Tis So Sweet to Trust in Jesus." Hymnary.org. https://hymnary.org/hymn/TTvirt/238 (accessed February 26, 2019).

23 Bill Adler, *comp.*, *Ask Billy Graham* (Nashville, TN: Thomas Nelson, 2012), 224.

24 Corrie Ten Boom with John and Elizabeth Sherrill, *The Hiding Place* (New York, NY: Bantom Books, 1971), 217.

25 J. Lee Grady. "Corrie Ten Boom: A Legacy of Courage." CharismaMag.com. https://www.charismamag.com site-archives/24-uncategorised/9933-corrie-ten-boom-a-legacy-of-courage (accessed February 20. 2019).

26 *Ibid.*

SESSION TWO

27 *Merriam Webster, s.v.,* "Bold," accessed February 20, 2019, https://www.merri-am-webster.com/dictionary/bold.

28 "Boldness," accessed February 20, 2019, https://www.dictionary.com/browse/boldness?s=t.

29 Liz Vice. "Meet Liz." LizVice.com. https://www.lizvice.com/about (accessed February 21, 2019).

30 *Ibid.*

31 Kelli B. Trujillo. "She Shaped Me: 10 Exemplars of Faith." ChristianyToday.com. https://www.christianitytoday.com/women/2018/september/she-shaped-me-examplars-faith.html (accessed February 21, 2019).

32 *Ibid.*

33 Comfort and Lins, *eds., Life Application New Testament Commentary.*

34 Jim Cymbala, *Fresh Wind, Fresh Fire: What Happens When the Spirit of God Invades the Hearts of His People* (Grand Rapids, MI: Zondervan, 1997), 161.

35 Helen H. Lemmel. "Turn Your Eyes Upon Jesus." Hymnary.org. https://hymnary.org/hymn/BH1991/320 (accessed February 16, 2019).

36 *HCSB Study Bible* (Nashville, TN: Holman Bible Publishers, 2010), 1812.

37 Dandapati Samuel Satyaranjan, *The Preaching of Daniel Thambirajah (D.T.) Niles: Homiletical Criticism* (Delhi: Indian Society for Promoting Christian Knowledge, 2009).

38 William Lane Craig, *Reasonable Faith: Christian Truth and Apologetics* (Wheaton, IL: Crossway, 2008), 368.

39 Gerald L. Borchert, *The New American Commentary,* vol. 25b, *John 12-25* (Nashville, TN: Broadman & Holman, 2002), 297.

40 Margaret J. Wheatley, *Turning to One Another: Simple Conversations to Restore Hope to the Future* (San Francisco, CA: Berrett-Koehler Publishers, 2002), 145.

41 Rebecca Manley Pippert, *Out of the Saltshaker & into the World* (Downers Grove, IL: InterVarsity Press, 1999).

42 John B. Polhill, *The New American Commentary,* vol. 26, *Acts* (Nashville, TN: Broadman & Holman, 1992).

43 Pippert, *Out of the Saltshaker & into the World.*

44 *Ibid.*

45 *Ibid.*

46 Polhill, *Acts.*

47 Jon Bloom. "Lord, Make Me More Bold." DesiringGod.org. https://www.desiringgod.org/articles/lord-make-me-more-bold (accessed February 18, 2019).

48 Brandon Showalter. "Francis Chan Urges Believers to Reject 'Cop-Out' Christianity, Lose Your Life for the Gospel." ChristianPost.com. https://www.christianpost.com/news/francis-chan-calls-on-believers-reject-cop-out-christianity-lose-your-life-for-the-gospel.html (accessed February 18, 2019).

49 *Ibid.*

50 Barna Group. "Almost Half of Practicing Christian Millennials Say Evangelism Is Wrong." Barna.com. https://www.barna.com/research/

millennials-oppose-evangelism/
(accessed March 19, 2019).
51 Samuel Smith. "Francis Chan:
Christians Will Be Relevant If
They Become Rejects, Stand With
Jesus." ChristianPost.com. https://
www.christianpost.com/news/
francis-chan-together-2016-chris-
tians-relevant-rejects-jesus-166599/
(accessed February 18, 2019).

SESSION THREE
52 Katie Davis, *Kisses From Katie* (New
York, NY: Howard Books, 2011).
53 Adapted from "No Ordinary Life: Katie
Davis' Story of Serving Children in
Uganda," by Ande Fanning, Summer
2011, *Collegiate Magazine*, p. 20.
Copyright 2011 by LifeWay Christian
Resources. Adapted with permission.
54 Chad Brand, Charles Draper, and
Archie England, eds., "Compassion" in
The Holman Illustrated Bible Dictionary
(Nashville, TN: Holman Bible
Publishers, 2003), 324.
55 *Ibid.*
56 Robert H. Stein, *The New American
Commentary*, vol. 24, *Luke* (Broadman
& Holman, 1992).
57 Pass It On. "Sent 19 Poor Kids to
College." PassItOn.com. https://www.
passiton.com/inspirational-sayings-bill-
boards/21-helping-others (accessed
February 19, 2019).
58 *Ibid.*
59 Oral Lee Brown Foundation.
"Who Is Oral Lee Brown?"
OralLeeBrownFounrdation.org. https://
www.oralleebrownfoundation.org/
(accessed February 19, 2019)
60 *Ibid.*
61 David M. Howard, Jr., The New
American Commentary, vol. 5, Joshua
(Nashville, TN: Broadman & Holman,
1998).

SESSION FOUR
62 George Mueller, *Answers to Prayer*
(Alachua, FL: Bridge-Logos, 2013).
63 George Mueller, as quoted by Henry
T. Blackaby and Richard Blackaby,
*Spiritual Leadership: Moving People on
to God's Agenda* (Nashville, TN: B&H
Publishing Group, 2001), 152.
64 *Ibid.*
65 Robert D. Bergen *The New American
Commentary*, vol. 7, *1, 2 Samuel*
(Broadman & Holman, 1996), 71.
66 *Ibid.*
67 *Ibid.*, 58.
68 *Ibid.*, 61.
69 Timothy Keller, *Prayer: Experiencing
Awe and Intimacy with God* (New York,
NY: Penguin, 2014), 228.
70 *HCSB Study Bible*, 2005.
71 Kelli B. Trujillo. "After 50 Years in a
Wheelchair, I Still Walk with Jesus."
ChristianityToday.com. https://www.
christianitytoday.com/women/2017/
july/joni-eareckson-tada-fifty-years-
wheelchair-walk-jesus.html (accessed
February 19, 2019).
72 *Ibid.*
73 Philip Yancey, as quoted by Joni
Eareckson Tada, *More Precious Than
Silver* (Grand Rapids, MI: Zondervan,
1998).
74 Thomas Edison, as quoted by Dustin
Ahlers, *The Ride We Call Life* (Lulu.com,
2014).
75 *Ibid.*
76 John Piper, *Don't Waste Your Life*
(Wheaton, IL: CrossWay, 2004).
77 The Nobel Prize. "Mother Teresa."
NobelPrize.org. https://www.nobelprize.
org/prizes/peace/1979/teresa/biograph-
ical/ (accessed February 20, 2019).
78 Renzo Allegri. "Mother Teresa Wasn't
Afraid to Die." Zenit.org. https://zenit.
org/articles/mother-teresa-wasn-t-
afraid-to-die/ (accessed February 20,
2019).

79 *Ibid.*

80 *Ibid.*

81 Comfort and Lins, *eds., Life Application New Testament Commentary.*

82 Eugene H. Peterson, *Long Obedience in the Same Direction: Discipleship in an Instant Society* (Downers Grove, IL: IVP Books, 1980), 133.

83 Billy Graham, *Hope for Each Day: Words of Wisdom and Faith* (Nashville, TN: Thomas Nelson, 2002), 112.

84 C. S. Lewis, *The Complete C. S. Lewis Signature Classics* (New York, NY: Harper Collins, 2017).

SESSION FIVE

85 Suzanne Pullen. "The Jefferson Award: Carol Donald, foster-care mom." SFGate.com. https://www.sfgate.com/bayarea/article/The-Jefferson-Award-Carol-Donald-foster-care-mom-2644967.php (accessed February 20, 2019).

86 Pass It On. "Fostered Good Will. And 100 Kids." PassItOn.com. https://www.passiton.com/inspirational-sayings-billboards/30-love (accessed February 20, 2019).

87 *HCSB Study Bible,* 1709.

88 Randy Newman. *You've Got a Friend in Me* (Burbank: Walt Disney, 1996).

89 Woodrow Wilson. "Address to the Citizenship Convention at Wilson Normal School." Presidency.ucsb.edu. http://www.presidency.ucsb.edu/ws/index.php?pid=117700 (accessed February 20, 2019).

90 *Merriam Webster, s.v.,* "Selfless," accessed February 20, 2019, https://www.merriam-webster.com/dictionary/selfless.

91 *Merriam Webster, s.v.,* "Self-sacrifice," accessed February 20, 2019, https://www.merriam-webster.com/dictionary/self-sacrifice.

SESSION SIX

92 C. H. Spurgeon, *Sermons of the Rev. C. H. Spurgeon, of London, Third Series* (New York, NY: Sheldon, Blakeman, & Company, 1858).

93 Scott LaFee. "Researchers Develop New Tool to Assess Individual's Level of Wisdom." Health.ecsd.edu. https://health.ucsd.edu/news/releases/Pages/2017-09-20-researchers-develop-new-tool-to-assess-wisdom.aspx (accessed February 20, 2019).

94 "Deborah" in *The Holman Illustrated Bible Dictionary,* 408.

95 Bill Gates. "A Teacher Who Changed My Life." GatesNotes.com. https://www.gatesnotes.com/Education/A-Teacher-Who-Changed-My-Life (accessed February 21, 2019).

96 *Ibid.*

97 *Ibid.*